1974

FOR THE FIRST HOURS OF TOMORROW

This book may be kept

FOURTEEN DAYS

A fine will be charged for each day the book is kept overtime.

STUDIES IN ILLINOIS CONSTITUTION MAKING
Joseph P. Pisciotte, *Editor*

For the First Hours
of Tomorrow: The New
Illinois Bill of Rights

ELMER GERTZ

Published for the
INSTITUTE OF GOVERNMENT AND PUBLIC AFFAIRS
by the
UNIVERSITY OF ILLINOIS PRESS
Urbana   Chicago   London

*Special appreciation is expressed to
the Field Foundation of Illinois,
whose financial support has made
this series possible.*

For Mamie,
a true friend to each member
of the Bill of Rights Committee
and all who participated in the convention

Take them both, love,
The book and me together.
Where the heart lies
Let the brain lie also.

— ROBERT BROWNING

Contents

Foreword

An increasing number of academic and participant observers are becoming sharply aware of the absence of a significant body of literature dealing with the processes of state constitutional revision. Awareness of this void has quickened recently as citizens and governmental officials in more and more states have taken an interest in various forms of constitutional revision.

The National Municipal League has led the field in developing what literature does exist, but even their efforts — a valuable beginning — have dealt only with such topics as the need for reform and the means of effecting constitutional revision once the need is realized. Recently, while continuing to serve as a clearinghouse of information, the League has gone a step further and sponsored individual studies of most of the state constitutional conventions since 1940. These studies fall into the same category as most of the other writings on state constitutional revision, that is, they are descriptive and analytic and reflect the viewpoint of only one observer. In each instance the reader is forced to accept the conclusions of one writer using one particular method of analysis.

Many still feel the need for more probing analyses to deal with questions which are answered now mostly by speculation. For example, we know very little about the impact of demographic variables, urbanization, or party on the outcome of elections required to initiate or implement revisions. We are not certain as to the advantages or disadvantages of partisan versus nonpartisan conventions. We are unsure about how best to organize and operate conventions, and to present a proposed change to the voters. We have yet to analyze fully alternative methods of selecting public officials and the resulting outputs of the agency or department involved, and most importantly, we have not yet begun accurately to assess the role of constitutional reform in state government and politics. Although we generally accept the premise that reform is needed, we are not certain of its impact, if any, on social and political change. Some have argued that constitutional reform is more symbolic than substantive, and that its effect is determined by other forces at work on decision making in state and local government.

The recently concluded Sixth Illinois Constitutional Convention provided observers an excellent opportunity to study the constitutional revision process. The Institute of Government and Public Affairs of the University of Illinois has authorized the writing and publication of a series of monographs, Studies in Illinois Constitution Making, which examine the Illinois convention and attempt to deal with some of the unanswered questions about state constitutional revision. Each study treats a specific phase of the revision process and is written by authors who had a close relationship to the convention in one of several capacities. The studies display a variety of methodologies in their analyses and conclusions.

The primary aim of the series is to recount — in breadth and detail — the events, personalities, strategies, conflicts, and resolutions which resulted in a new basic law for Illinois. Neither the convention nor these studies were conducted in isolation from the political environment of the state, hence, the first of several secondary goals of the series is to contribute to the general knowledge of the politics of Illinois. It is also our aim to provide a basis for later studies dealing with the implementation and impact of the new document. And finally, it is our hope that the series will lend itself to comparative studies on state constitutional revision and ultimately to the development of descriptive and theoretical literature in this area.

The Institute expresses its deep appreciation to the Field Foundation of Illinois which recognized the need for these studies and provided the funding for them. In each study the statements and views expressed are solely the responsibility of the author.

JOSEPH P. PISCIOTTE,
Series Editor

SAMUEL K. GOVE,
Institute Director

Introduction

This is not a conventional monograph. Convention would have it exhaustive, impersonal, and dull. Those who know Elmer Gertz, chairman of the Bill of Rights Committee of the Sixth Illinois Constitutional Convention, would not expect his monograph to be conventional.

Elmer Gertz has written a vivid and vital *biography* of the Bill of Rights Committee. His treatment is worthy of the subject. And what a subject it was! Whether by design or by inadvertence, President Samuel W. Witwer's appointments to the Bill of Rights Committee assembled what was easily the most remarkable group of delegates at the Constitutional Convention. The working relationships and accomplishments of this unusually diverse group of people are a story that deserves to be told. It is well that the chairman of this group has the insight and literary talents to tell the story as only an insider can tell it.

Elmer Gertz is a shrewd and dispassionate observer. Although his manner of writing is highly personal — even self-centered — he has the uncommon virtue of seeing others clearly. From his highly personal style of writing, which presents everyone in a satellite-type relationship to the writer, one might expect a good deal of bias in the observations and evaluations of others. Not so with this monograph, which strikes this interested observer as remarkably objective and admirably fair.

The Bill of Rights Committee gave distinguished service to the people of Illinois. Though one may disagree with some provisions in the finished product, the new bill of rights is an admirable document,

worthy of study and emulation. This monograph will be a valuable
and fascinating aid for persons who want to understand the political
and personal process that produced this vital article of the new
Illinois Constitution.

DALLIN H. OAKS*
President
February 8, 1972   Brigham Young University

* Legal and Research Advisor to the Bill of Rights Committee, January–June,
1970, while on leave as a Professor of Law, The University of Chicago.

Acknowledgments

Even in a monograph that strives to be original and personal, there is evidence on every page of great indebtedness to many persons. Although I have no desire to absolve myself from complete responsibility for what is said in these pages, simple justice requires that I thank those who have been of help to me.

First and foremost of those I must thank is Dr. Joseph P. Pisciotte, Executive Director of the Sixth Illinois Constitutional Convention and editor of the series of monographs of which the present book is a part. Dr. Pisciotte almost instantly complied with my every request, reasonable or unreasonable, whether it was for transcripts of the convention proceedings, pertinent documents, research, suggestions, or typing.

Then I must thank my wife, Mamie Gertz, for arranging the great number of news articles of the convention and my committee in organized, chronological and useable form, and for giving me her impressions, from time to time, of what I wrote.

Certain of the delegates were good enough to give me their recollections of important issues or material that was of help to me, either as background or for direct use — Mrs. Virginia B. Macdonald, Lewis D. Wilson, Clifford L. Downen, Ralph A. Dunn, Dwight P. Friedrich, John M. Karns, Jr., and David E. Stahl.

The media people, particularly the newspaper correspondents, were invaluable, both directly and indirectly. I think especially of John Elmer and Edith Herman of the *Chicago Tribune,* Charles Wheeler III of the *Chicago Sun-Times,* Edward S. Gilbreth and John Camper of the *Chicago Daily News,* Malden Jones of *Chicago*

Today, and various downstate journalists. My dear friend, Charles McCuen, formerly of NBC, now of the Department of Public Instruction, gave me knowledge and insight and encouragement throughout the convention and since then. Throughout these pages, I quote from newspaper articles, for which I must acknowledge my indebtedness.

I must thank my friend Louis Ancel for counseling and aiding me at times when his help was truly needed.

Through Dr. Pisciotte, I had the research assistance of J. D. Bindenagel and the editorial assistance of Mrs. Ashley Nugent. Their work is acknowledged with appreciation.

My secretaries, Deborah Klayman and Claudia Corell, did excellent jobs of first-draft typing and supplied helpful comments.

One chapter of this work consists largely of a paraphrase of the report of the Bill of Rights Committee, stemming from Dallin H. Oaks, the invaluable special counsel of the committee. Another chapter consists largely of paraphrases of the minority reports. No one deserves more credit for these than Bernard Weisberg.

And throughout the writing and thinking about this work, I was cognizant every moment of that very remarkable group of persons who made up the Bill of Rights Committee. They are unforgettable. I pay my respects to them, in specific terms, in the ensuing pages. And I want to thank convention President Samuel W. Witwer for his faith in me.

ELMER GERTZ

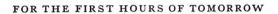

FOR THE FIRST HOURS OF TOMORROW

I

First Principles

In the spring of 1924 I was about to graduate from high school, and I neared my eighteenth birthday. My father being ill one day, I was in charge of his clothing store on the South Side of Chicago. Two big men entered the store. At first glance, they looked like hoodlums, and I feared they were going to rob me. One of them said peremptorily, "Come with us, kid!" I asked the reason, and they declined to answer. I asked if I could call my father, and they refused. They took me in their automobile to the northwest side of the city to a police station, miles from my father's store, and left me, unattended, in a locked room. After a time, another man entered the room; I took him to be a plainclothes detective. He got into a conversation with me on the subject that was on everyone's mind and tongue, the Loeb-Leopold case, which had just broken. The young men who had kidnapped and murdered the Franks boy were not much older than I was. They, like me, were Jewish and South Siders; they were at the end of their academic careers at the University of Chicago, and I was about to begin mine there. The officer must have thought that this gave me special competence on the subject. We talked for hours, each speculating why such things should occur. I was given no food or drink; I was held incommunicado.

Suddenly, around midnight, the officer said: "Kid, you can call your father." He also told me, for the first time, that I was being held because a stolen negotiable bond was traced to me. I had deposited one of its interest coupons in my savings account. The only bond I owned had been given to me as a gift in anticipation of my graduation. I knew nothing about its being stolen, nor did the one who had given it to me, I learned later. I explained the situation to my troubled father and he attempted to persuade a judge whom we knew to order my release. The judge was rather annoyed that he was called so late. "Can't your son remain in jail over night?" he asked. Finally, he arranged for my release. The next morning I appeared before another judge. Learning about the situation, he laughed and quickly discharged me; and that was the end, so far as the majestic state was concerned.

I did not know then how many constitutional rights of mine had been breached by this outrageous incident, even by the standards of that day. I could now add up a dozen or so. I was sure then, as now, that many people, young and old, educated and uneducated, white and black, had been subjected to the same, or worse, treatment. At least I had not been beaten up and my travail, such as it was, had been relatively brief. With one part of my brain, I had enjoyed it. Then as now, new experiences intrigued me.

I am sure too that I became a lawyer, rather than an architect or journalist, to which I aspired in almost equal degrees, because I wanted to make certain that fundamental rights would be preserved for all people, and that I would have a share in the great task. The same feeling prompted me to become a founder of the first multi-racial literary society at the University of Chicago and to participate in every effort to create a brotherly community. All my life I have been devoted to enhancement of the Bill of Rights. To me it is authentic Scripture, no less than the Pentateuch. My law practice, my writings, my public and private activities have been a crusade, if the word is not impious, against infringements of constitutional rights. This dedication impelled me to run for election as a delegate to the Sixth Illinois Constitutional Convention. I wanted to help make certain that the bill of rights would not be weakened in this period in which fundamental rights are too often conversational, rather than operative.

Winning an unexpected victory, I found myself, even more unexpectedly, chairman of the Bill of Rights Committee. There followed nine months of the most rewarding endeavors in a not uneventful life. This is the story of those months, in part a personal tale, in part the story of clashes between principles and personalities. I have tried to make clear the meanings of what we produced, as well as how our achievements were accomplished. In the framework of a highly human tale, I have not neglected the hard core of constitutional doctrine. Here is a little book for every citizen on a subject that should be as dear to him as the bread and meat of his daily life. I hope that through this endeavor, I will have carried forward the inspiring work that began publicly one day early in December 1969 and ended with the adoption of the new constitution one year later. For me the story really began in the spring of 1924 and will never end.

Those charged with responsibility for a bill of rights article at the Sixth Illinois Constitutional Convention would be asked, at the outset and repeatedly, about the relationship of such an article to the first ten amendments and the Fourteenth Amendment to the United States Constitution. The prime questions would be: What do those federal amendments provide? And why are they not sufficient for all purposes here in Illinois? Legitimate questions these, and they were faced firmly during the nine months following the opening session of the convention.

It will be remembered that ratification of the federal constitution was conditional in those early days of the Republic upon the prompt adoption of a bill of rights. That is what the first ten amendments, taken collectively, represent.

It would seem that all Americans, young and old, are familiar with them; but they always have a ring of grandeur, no matter how often repeated.

The first characteristics of these familiar rights are that they are in general terms and are grouped together, several rights in each section; few of the rights are particularized. And they are ancient in origin and often in phraseology; Magna Carta, the Great Charter, exacted by the barons from King John at Runnymede in England these many centuries ago, spelled out what has become law in the United States, especially since the Fourteenth Amendment has been expanded in meaning and scope, and the Supreme Court has increasingly decreed that what was once binding only upon the federal Union is now equally binding upon the states, including Illinois, of course.

Thus the First Amendment — the very words suggest rights too sacred to be abridged — includes (a) religious freedom, (b) separation of church and state, (c) freedom of speech and press, (d) peaceable assembly, and (e) petition for redress of grievances. It is at once apparent that other state constitutions, including ours, have attenuated this text, so that, for better or for worse, it requires several sections and much additional language.

The Second Amendment is the collective right of the people, through a militia, to keep and bear arms.

The Third Amendment relates to the quartering of soldiers in private houses, forbidden in peace, limited by law in war.

The security of the people against unreasonable searches and seizures is protected in the Fourth Amendment.

Then the five subjects of (a) grand jury indictments for infamous crimes, (b) double jeopardy, (c) self-incrimination, (d) due process of law, and (e) taking of private property for public use — these are all covered in the famous Fifth Amendment, the foundation of much grandeur and some infamy in our national life.

In the Sixth Amendment, again, a variety of rights in all criminal prosecutions are declared — (a) the right to a speedy and public trial by an impartial jury as therein defined, (b) the right to be informed of the nature and cause of the accusation, (c) the right to compulsory process for witnesses, and (d) the right to assistance of counsel. It should be observed that with this amendment, as with the First and Fifth, at least five distinct rights of all persons are spelled out in phrases that have been interpreted and reinterpreted by the courts in innumerable cases and by commentators in countless treatises and tomes. The literature is literally limitless, more so even than in the generations of Talmudists who have spelled out the meanings of each syllable and letter of Holy Scripture.

The right to trial by jury in suits at common law is declared in the Seventh Amendment.

The Eighth Amendment, even more than some of the others, is one of expanding meaning and applicability, and prohibits excessive bail, excessive fines, and cruel and unusual punishments.

The Ninth and Tenth Amendments declare, respectively, that the rights not enumerated are retained by the people and the powers not delegated to the United States are reserved to the states or to the people.

It takes just about a page to set forth the federal Bill of Rights, recognized everywhere as the foundation of our security as a free people. Then came the three amendments born out of the agony, death, and destruction of the Civil War. One of these three, the Fourteenth, has made the first ten amendments visible, viable, and indestructible. This amendment does many things in each of its five sections, but it is the first section that most concerned those chosen to consider anew the constitution of Illinois. By it we were constrained not to abridge the privileges or immunities of any citizen of the United States and not to deprive any person of life, liberty, or property without due process of law, nor deny the equal protection of the laws.

Anyone reading the Illinois Bill of Rights, Article II of the 1870 constitution, is aware at once that many of these rights are spelled out in various sections, often with the same verbiage as in the federal constitution and sometimes in expanded terms or with different phraseology.

There had been no great demand for a changed bill of rights when the people of Illinois voted overwhelmingly to call a constitutional convention. People were generally pleased, as well they might be, with what we had. In some quarters there was a fear that change would be for the worse, rather than the better; that there was the danger of going backward, rather than forward. The first phrase of caution for all of us was, therefore, "Stop, look, and listen." That did not mean simply surrendering our right and duty to review the whole constitutional document, from the preamble to the certification. Review meant looking at various documents and treatises, hearing from those with views on the fundamental rights, considering all the proposals presented to us.

There were some basic documents and studies more important than others. These were the first things that were to come first, as the old cliché has it.

All persons concerned with constitutional revision, whether pertaining to the bill of rights or any other part of a basic charter, must

consult the Model State Constitution, the collective effort of many
legal scholars and practitioners under the auspices of the National
Municipal League.[1] Virtually all members of the Bill of Rights Committee, one may be sure, consulted this invaluable document from
time to time. Together with the Braden and Cohn treatise and the
work of the Illinois Constitution Research Group, it was the nearly
indispensable prelude to action. Later in the life of the committee,
only the memoranda prepared by the committee counsel and his
young researchers had more value. At the outset, when there were
no such memoranda, the Model State Constitution filled many needs
for both the lawyer and lay members. Yet the introduction to this
important document begins with a disclaimer: "Strictly speaking
there can be no such thing as a 'Model State Constitution' because
there is no model state." Moreover, the ideal state would probably
need no written constitution. The suggestions were traditional, rather
than revolutionary or radical, in conformity to basic American political ideas, including, of course, those held by the citizens of Illinois.
Still it resembled the constitutions of the newer states, such as those
of Alaska and Hawaii, rather than the older ones. Its aim was simplicity and clarity. It sought to eliminate overelaboration and purely
statutory provisions or much that smacked of a lack of confidence
in government.

This became apparent at once in the model preamble — six lines
reciting that the state is part of the federal system and must therefore adhere to the federal constitution, and that the purpose of the
state constitution is simply to assure "power to act for the good
order of the state and the liberty, health, safety and welfare of the
people. . . ."

All state constitutions, except those of Vermont and West Virginia, have preambles. The Illinois Constitution of 1870 certainly
was more elaborate than suggested by the model code. No state constitution, including the Illinois Constitution of 1870 and those of
earlier years, acknowledged the obvious membership in a federal
system. Would we who were to produce the 1970 constitution proclaim this fact? Would we compress the 1870 preamble to the size
and shape of the model, or would we be even more elaborate and

[1] National Municipal League, *Model State Constitution* (New York, 1963,
1968).

eloquent? And would we use modern language or the more traditional language?

Then there were the operative provisions of the Model State Constitution Bill of Rights, few in number and briefly expressed. There
was, in the very first section, a one sentence statement with respect
to the freedom of religion, speech, press, assembly, and petition,
largely in the language of the First Amendment of the Constitution
of the United States and common to virtually every state constitution,
however much the specific language differed. These matters were
covered by several sections of the 1870 constitution of Illinois —
section 3, a long statement in the bill of rights on religious freedom,
carefully defining it, and a long statement in the education article
forbidding public funds for sectarian purposes; section 4 in the bill
of rights on freedom of speech, with a special statement as to libel;
and section 17, as to the right to assemble and petition. Would these
be consolidated, abbreviated, and modernized, with non-essentials
eliminated?

The next section of the model code related to due process and
equal protection: "No person shall be deprived of life, liberty or
property without due process of law, nor be denied the equal protection of the laws, nor be denied the enjoyment of his civil rights or
be discriminated against in the exercise thereof because of race,
national origin, religion or ancestry." The familiar terminology of
the first two clauses, due process and equal protection of the laws,
followed the Fifth and Fourteenth Amendments of the United States
Constitution. The first, the due process clause, could be found in
virtually every state constitution, including the Illinois Constitution
of 1870. The rest of the language of the section did not appear in
the Illinois Constitution of 1870, but it was generally believed, and
seemed to be established by the cases, that equal protection of the
laws was assured by the Fourteenth Amendment and did not necessarily have to be spelled out in a state charter; and that the final
clause, on civil rights, sounded very well indeed, but granted no
right not already implicit in due process and equal protection. Yet
much could be said for inclusion of all of the language of the section, if only for the sake of completeness. Would the committee and
and the convention go that far, or even further?

Then came a section in the model code on searches and seizures and interceptions, in three paragraphs. The first paragraph, inhibiting unreasonable searches and seizures, followed the Fourth Amendment of the federal constitution and could be found in the constitution of almost every state, including Illinois (section 6 of the 1870 Illinois Bill of Rights). It was necessarily applicable to the states, including Illinois, by the Fourteenth Amendment. The second paragraph, not found in the Illinois Constitution of 1870, on interceptions of communications, was based on a clause on wiretapping in the New York Constitution. It followed the pattern of the first paragraph on searches and seizures by permitting court orders in restricted circumstances, and this might have tended in practice to water down any good effect flowing from the general ban. The third paragraph, also not found in the Illinois Bill of Rights of 1870, banned evidence obtained in violation of the first two paragraphs, a result assured, at least with respect to the usual search and seizure, by the Fourteenth Amendment.

As the Illinois convention began, it was clear that the general theme of invasions of privacy and interceptions of communications would receive much consideration. The question was: Would the committee and the convention follow the lead of New York, or go beyond it? Would there, for example, be an absolute ban on interceptions of communications, or a conditional one? Would the Illinois statute, permitting single-party consent for wiretapping, be constitutionalized or limited in any way?

The next section of the Model State Constitution, following the language and intent of the federal constitution and those of most, if not all, of the states including Illinois (second clause of section 7), declared the writ of habeas corpus could not be suspended unless rebellion, invasion, or the public safety required it. There was slight question about this provision being included in the bill of rights of any new constitution. It was simply a commonplace, over which there would be little, if any, discussion.

The following section, on the rights of accused persons, lumped together some language of the Sixth, Eighth, and Fourteenth Amendments and at least one federal rule of criminal procedure, a statute or two, and the holdings of several landmark cases. The provisions as to a speedy and public trial could be found in almost all of the state constitutions, including that of Illinois (last clauses of section 9). This was true also of the language as to being informed as to the nature and cause of the accusation (section 9, also). It was less true — that is, fewer state constitutions had provisions — as to the accused being entitled to a copy of the charge. It was incorporated in section 9 (rights after indictment) of the 1870 Illinois Bill of Rights article. The provision as to compulsory process to obtain witnesses was found in all of the state constitutions, except those of Nevada and, strangely enough, New York. It too was part of section 9 of the 1870 Illinois Bill of Rights. As to the right to counsel, only Virginia's of all the state constitutions lacked this; but it was, in any event, the law of the land since the famous case of *Gideon* v. *Wainwright*[2] and subsequent United States Supreme Court decisions. The provision as to excessive bail was found in all of the state constitutions, except those of Illinois and Vermont. The rest of the bail provision was found in the constitutions of forty of the states, including Illinois (the first clause of section 7 and section 11; the rest of the section dealing with habeas corpus). The provision as to cruel or unusual punishment, required by the Eighth Amendment, was found in all of the state constitutions except those of Connecticut and again Illinois. Finally, the provision as to double jeopardy was found either identically or in substance in all of the state constitutions except Connecticut, Vermont, and Georgia. It was found in section 10 of the 1870 Illinois Bill of Rights, coupled with the privilege against self-incrimination.

Just to recite these various rights suffices to indicate that, as a matter of course, any constitutional convention would adopt them in one form or other. With respect to Illinois, it might be asked whether the omitted language, such as that with respect to cruel or unusual punishment or excessive bail, would be added to the bill of rights, or would the convention be content to confine itself to the time-honored language already in the constitution and interpreted substantially the same, despite any omissions or differences in the text?

The model code bill of rights closed with a provision that no oath, declaration, or political test was required for public office or employment other than support of the federal and state constitutions

---

[2] 372 U.S. 335, 83 S. Ct. 792, 9 L. Ed. 2h 799 (1963).

and faithful discharge of duties. While the provision was not in the Illinois Bill of Rights, a somewhat similar version of it could be found elsewhere in the Illinois Constitution of 1870. It was a virtual certainty that the same subject matter would be covered by any new constitution.

Nothing other than these enumerated provisions was included in the bill of rights of the Model State Constitution. There were no provisions similar to what was found in the 1870 Illinois Bill of Rights in section 1 (inherent and inalienable rights), section 12 (imprisonment for debt), section 13 (right of eminent domain), section 14 (ex post facto laws and impairing contracts), section 15 (subordination of military power), section 16 (quartering of soldiers), section 18 (free elections), section 19 (right to remedy and justice), and section 20 (fundamental principles). Would the convention regard all of these sections as necessary or expedient? Would their language be modified for the sake of clarity and simplicity? Would any additional rights or obligations of government or individuals be spelled out? There was little room for preconception or cocksureness. Much would depend, in the first instance, upon the personalities and principles of the members of the Bill of Rights Committee, the staff, the witnesses, the documents presented for consideration. There was no assurance that the convention as a whole would necessarily ratify what any of its committees proposed.

Any bill of rights produced by the convention would be judged in the context of the federal Bill of Rights and the Fourteenth Amendment. We could not secede from the Union. We were bound by the law of the land. Whether we chose to comply or not, most of our individual rights stemmed from the federal tree. But our state bill of rights might perform important functions. We might go beyond what was required by the Fourteenth Amendment; we could not give our citizens less, but we could give them more. Would we?

Some at any convention play — and vote — by ear, or by direction. Others are independent, thoughtful, dedicated. All are creatures of their social and individual chemistries. It would be interesting and possibly rewarding to observe.

Governor Richard B. Ogilvie caused a series of research papers prepared by the Constitution Research Group to be sent to all of the delegates both before and during the convention.[3] The governor stressed that he did not necessarily agree with all that was said by the various members of the group; he wanted "to stimulate independent thinking, not to write a draft of a proposed constitution." Two of the papers dealt with problems to come before the Bill of Rights Committee, and an additional paper constituted a general introduction to constitution making and contained much material about the Illinois Bill of Rights. There was thus more material in our sphere than in any other. The more dedicated members of our committee read these papers and probably the whole series; for while we had primary responsibility for the bill of rights, we had coequal power with all delegates to frame an entirely new constitution, if we should choose to submit a complete general revision rather than separate amendments. We were given the case for brevity — the briefer and more compact, the more likely it was "to be read, studied, and understood." The whole constitution was reduced to certain fundamentals — "the frame of government, the declaration of rights, and the amending process." Thus we on the Bill of Rights Committee were given a basic assignment as to one-third of the total conceptual goal; Peter Tomei's committee on suffrage, elections, and amending, another third; and all of the other substantive committees the remaining third! Of course, this is oversimplification, but that would be the least of our considerations. Others would tell us not to change a jot or a tittle of the total.

It was pointed out by Professor Paul G. Kauper that the earliest English and American constitutional documents were chiefly statements of the rights of individuals against arbitrary and despotic acts of the government — what was incorporated in the 1870 Illinois Bill of Rights, as well as the Bill of Rights and Fourteenth Amendment of the federal constitution. It was made clear why the federally protected rights were not enough, extensive though they were in some important respects. There was in them nothing that went quite as far as sections 1 (fundamental rights), 3 (religious freedom), 13 (eminent domain), and 19 (right to remedy and justice)

---

[3] These papers were later published as *Con-Con: Issues for the Illinois Constitutional Convention,* ed. by Samuel K. Gove and Victoria Ranney (Urbana: University of Illinois Press, 1970). References are made in the next several pages to the first three articles in the book, those by Paul G. Kauper, by Frank P. Grad, and by Lucius J. Barker and Twiley W. Barker, Jr.

of the 1870 Illinois Bill of Rights. Besides, the Illinois Supreme
Court might give the provisions in our bill of rights an interpretation
transcending that declared by the United States Supreme Court.
And a bill of rights could arrest, in some respects, the excessive
trend towards federal centralization of power.

Again, it was pointed out that when the old words are used, the
courts tend to interpret the provision as in the past. What, then,
happens to the goal of simplifying the document? Is there not an
argument for the retention of the language of the old sections, and
revising this language only when one wants to make substantive
changes in the old rights or to add brand new rights consonant with
the modern tendency to extend civil rights, for example? Might not
social and economic rights of a special nature be set forth, without
necessarily creating a welfare state or complicating the structure of
government? To what extent should the rights of citizens against
other citizens be specified, or should the bill of rights pertain only
to the rights of citizens vis-à-vis the state?

Professor Frank P. Grad pointed out, briefly, what Professors
Braden and Cohn spelled out in detail in their commentary: that
the provisions of the 1870 bill of rights were all derived from the
state constitution of 1848 with only a few verbal changes; that
eighteen of the twenty sections went back, indeed, to the 1818 constitution, Illinois's first constitution, the one with which it was admitted to the Union; and that there were no amendments to the
1870 bill of rights in the century following its adoption. Professor
Grad felt that our 1870 bill of rights was "well within the norm of
states' bills of rights generally." What neither Professor Grad nor
the other commentators observed was that, despite the hoary years
of the basic guarantees, they were ignored with respect to the race
held in servitude supposedly in the South alone. As I pointed out
in my study of the Black Code of Illinois, our laws prior to 1865
were almost as oppressive as any Black Code in any state south of
the Mason and Dixon line. The lesson in this is that traditional language must be reexamined by those drafting new constitutions in
order to make certain that the rights are truly operative for all. It
was apparent that those of us who believed in those rights would
have to disenthral ourselves, as Lincoln phrased it, so that we would
accomplish what we professed and what was proclaimed so elo-

quently but ineffectively in the Declaration of Independence, almost two hundred years old as we began our deliberations.

What more could be said about freedom of expression in order to make certain that we — all of us — truly had such freedom? What more could be said about freedom of religion and its corollary separation of church and state in order to guard against encroachments, subtle or gross? And how could we assure due process and equal protection of the laws, so that we had not verbalisms but realities, secure against the most authoritarian officials? There were all of the vital regions covered by the 1870 bill of rights; each section would have to be studied for errors and omissions. There were new rights to be considered. Was the right to organize and bargain collectively to be set forth in a new section? Should we, perhaps, consider the so-called right to work, or was it a false issue, dangerous in its implications? And what about the Four Freedoms, proclaimed so sonorously by the immortal Franklin D. Roosevelt? Were they or any omissions in them to be spelled out by us? Were we to provide for the basic needs of all citizens "from the cradle to the grave," or at least for the "one-third of the nation" that lacked these assurances of the minimum needs?

And this led to the area of the guarantee of civil rights, discussed in the papers not by one professor, but by two — Lucius J. Barker and Twiley W. Barker, Jr. Few state constitutions covered this area adequately. Those who questioned whether it was a constitutional matter could be referred to the inadequacies in Illinois legislation. There was the old civil rights statute, breached more often than observed; more modern legislation on employment discrimination, limited both in scope and in enforcement; and there was the complete inability to get open housing laws. How, then, could we achieve progress in these areas constitutionally?

During the course of this monograph I refer to the monumental treatise by George D. Braden and Rubin G. Cohn — *The Illinois Constitution: An Annotated and Comparative Analysis*. It was published by the Institute of Government and Public Affairs of the University of Illinois in October 1969, even before delegates to the convention were elected. Distributed to all delegates, it was the single document most frequently consulted by the members of the Bill of

Rights Committee. Perhaps one-sixth of the entire book dealt with the area of our work. In addition, we had the privilege of a lengthy session with Professor Cohn at one of the very first meetings of our committee, during which he took us through the entire article that was to be the subject of our inquiry for months thereafter. He expounded and supplemented and clarified much that was said in the Braden-Cohn treatise, answered innumerable questions, and placed himself at our disposal then and thereafter. The chairman of the committee owes a very special debt of gratitude to Rubin G. Cohn, second only to his reliance, as we shall see, upon Professor Dallin H. Oaks. I felt at all times that I could rely upon Cohn for intimate counsel on the vast variety and multiplicity of problems that arose, and for solace, too, for my many wounds.

The Braden and Cohn book provided an analysis of each section of the 1870 constitution — a history of its development through past Illinois constitutions and constitutional conventions, including the ill-fated 1920–22 convention; an explanation of the meaning of each section, chiefly as determined by the cases, state and federal; a comparison with the like provisions in other state constitutions and the federal constitution; and, finally, a comment with recommendations for our consideration at the convention at which we were involved as delegates. Most of the responsibility for the analysis of the bill of rights article was Professor Cohn's; but as to some sections (15 — subordination of military power; 16 — quartering of soldiers; and 20 — fundamental principles) Professor Braden had responsibility.

One comment, at the outset of the book, was almost comical in its failure to gauge what might happen in our committee sessions. The learned authors opined: "Preambles have never evoked much political controversy and, strictly speaking, are not operative parts of a constitution."[4]

Braden and Cohn grouped together section 1 (inherent and inalienable rights) and section 20 (fundamental principles) as possibly valuable and certainly not harmful, and recommended retention of both provisions.

[4] George D. Braden and Rubin G. Cohn, *The Illinois Constitution: An Annotated and Comparative Analysis* (Urbana: Institute of Government and Public Affairs, University of Illinois, 1969). Quotations on the following several pages are taken from Braden and Cohn, pp. 1–65.

They thought that any suggestion to "delete or tamper with" section 2 (due process) would be viewed as "subversive." It could not be conceived, when they wrote these words, that some of the most conservative members of our committee would be the very ones to advocate tampering with this section, and that at least one member would look upon their recommendation for adding an equal protection of the laws provision as "revolutionary."

They thought it dangerous to meddle with section 3 (religious freedom), even though the simpler language of the First Amendment and the Model State Constitution had virtues.

They were receptive to eliminating or changing the words as to truth in libel actions in section 4 (freedom of speech).

In discussing section 5 (trial by jury), they understood the reasons for considering changes with respect to juries in civil cases, but cautioned: "The principle is, however, too important to be lightly treated, and no modification should be accepted which dilutes its political and psychological value."

On searches and seizures (section 6), they were conservative: "Every consideration of policy suggests that this principle be retained in the Illinois Constitution." We were soon to learn that there was a compelling course before us that included the retention of the old language, but dictated enlargements of it in areas not foreseen when the earlier constitutions were adopted.

They thought that we should consider "most cautiously any proposal which would diminish the existing right" to bail, and that there was no reason to justify repeal or modification of the provision with respect to habeas corpus (section 7).

They believed it unlikely that any rationale behind any change in the indictment provision (section 8) would secure general agreement, although they pointed out the basic contradiction in the section in purporting to preserve the institution while giving the legislature the power to abolish it.

Recognizing distinguished support for change in the privilege against self-incrimination (section 10), they yet felt that "given the psychological consensus that it commands, it would seem almost heretical to suggest that it be tampered with in any form." So as to double jeopardy, linked in section 10 to the aforementioned privilege, they were content to leave the matter to the normal evolutionary processes of the law, rather than to make verbal changes.

Section 11 (limitation of penalties after conviction) raised questions for Braden and Cohn. Should capital punishment be abolished constitutionally or left to the General Assembly? They were not sure. They were more certain about the archaic provisions as to corruption of blood and forfeiture of estate. They thought their abolition might seriously be considered, since federal and state due process were probably a sufficient protection against such sanctions.

While they recognized all sorts of difficulties with the provision on eminent domain (section 13) — "the many uncertainties, ambiguities and contradictions in the decisional law" — they felt, on balance, that "to tamper with the traditional language of this section may be productive of much harm." We ourselves would have one of the great debates of the convention on this section. The one point of agreement was, as suggested by Braden and Cohn, that the provision concerning railroads be deleted.

They believed that the provisions on ex post facto laws and contract impairment (section 14) should be retained as important limitations on state power, but should be tied in with the ban in the legislative article on special or local laws granting special privileges, franchises, or immunities and the limitation on the creation of corporations by special law.

The comments on the subordination of military power (section 15) and the quartering of soldiers (section 16) by Braden were a bit more abstruse than the comments on other sections, but might be translated to mean that there should be little tampering with the traditional language. They reached the same conclusion, less abstractly, with respect to retaining section 17 (right to assemble and petition), section 18 (free elections), and section 19 (right to remedy and justice). As to section 20 (fundamental principles), there were philosophical and constitutional doubts expressed, and the conclusion was voiced that there was no harm in retention, but the section might be combined with section 1 (inherent and inalienable rights).

Here, then, was the heart of the recommendations by two of our learned mentors. At various stages of the convention, they were present in advisory capacities — Braden with the Style and Drafting

Committee and Cohn with the Judiciary Committee. But, as they must sometimes have regretted, they had no votes and little voice. We, despite our limitations, were the ones to decide all things, subject in the end to the yea or nay of the convention and that of the sovereign People who might choose to vote on our final product.

II

The Personalities

On December 30, 1969, convention President Samuel W. Witwer announced his choices of committee chairmen and vice-chairmen in the State of Illinois Building in Chicago. The ladies and gentlemen entrusted with the new responsibilities were photographed and interviewed, and of course the newspapers and the media generally, particularly those in Chicago, reported the event. The *Chicago Tribune* story by John Elmer, from whom much would be heard during the course of the convention, said that the experts were surprised by some of Witwer's choices for the important posts, and that the regular Democratic organization of Cook County, under the supposedly omnipotent Mayor Daley, had fared badly. My appointment as chairman of the Bill of Rights Committee was referred to near the end of the article, where I was described as "a maverick Democrat," an epithet the *Tribune* used with respect to me for months afterwards. A few days later there came a full editorial blast at three of the new chairmen — John M. Karns, Jr., of the Revenue Committee, George J. Lewis of the Legislative Committee, and, above all, myself. Relatively mild as to Karns and Lewis, the *Tribune* sailed into me:

> A third puzzling appointment was that of Elmer Gertz, an independent Democrat from Chicago, to head the committee on the bill of rights. Mr. Gertz, a lawyer, has a long record as a noisy, ineffective busy-body. He can be counted on to use the committee to satisfy his itch for publicity.

The Illinois constitution now contains a perfectly good bill of rights. Many eminent citizens have urged that it be left as it is and labor leaders have warned that they will fight any changes. If the bill of rights committee turns its hearings into a hunting ground for ideological freaks and peddlers of utopian schemes, the whole Convention is likely to be discredited in the eyes of the voters.

The editorial closed with a prayer, as it were: "We hope the major committees, charged with the difficult jobs, will each be given members who have experience in the fields of study, as well as intelligence and good intentions. This is the only hope for practical recommendations from the convention."[1]

Thus revenged was my pamphlet, *The People v. The Chicago Tribune,* published in 1942 by the Union for Democratic Action and once called by "The World's Greatest Newspaper" the most scurrilous ever written. At the same time, *Chicago Today,* the afternoon paper owned by the *Tribune,* had special praise for the appointments of Peter A. Tomei, David E. Stahl, and myself as committee chairmen. Mine was the only name common to both lists. It would be an interesting seesaw to observe.

For many weeks thereafter the *Tribune* managed to place me in a dubious light while it reported both the antics and heroics of my committee at great length. I gave thought to the situation, not simply for my own sake, but because I owed a special debt to Samuel Witwer who had been besieged by the *Tribune* in the effort to prevent my appointment, and I had an obligation to the committee and the convention not to let mutual hostility imperil our work. I adopted a special course of conduct. As whenever I have been engaged in public activities in the past, I made certain that I treated *Tribune* reporters with the same courtesy and fairness that I extended to others. I acted as if I was unaware that their antipathy might distort what I said or did. At the same time, I carefully refrained from seeking out any reporters, whether the *Tribune*'s or others'. If they wanted information or interpretation, they would come to me, not me to them in the fashion of that distinguished press-minded delegate Paul Elward. Sometimes I had to use will

[1] "Witwer Picks Chairmen of Con-Con Units," *Chicago Tribune,* December 31, 1969.

power, for there were occasions when I might have fed helpful material to the media.

Then, to jump ahead happily, there came a time after the adoption of the constitution when the editors of the *Tribune* told me that they owed me an apology and that they had often regretted what they had said of me editorially. Had they changed, or had I? This belongs to my story, rather than to a narrative of the bill of rights. I must say, however, that gradually I did detect a change in the *Tribune*'s attitude, even before the apology, and I was given hints of developments high in the Tower.

Notwithstanding the *Tribune*'s criticism, there were some who thought that I was highly suited for the chairmanship because of my long association with the struggle for individual rights, my independent attitude, and my having attained the years of maturity. Others, not critical of me, felt that the younger man Bernard Weisberg, also a Chicago Independent and a long-time battler for constitutional rights, might be better suited for the task. A graduate with honors from the University of Chicago and *cum laude* from its law school, Phi Beta Kappa, Coif, managing editor of the law review, a graduate student in sociology and education, an accomplished musician, a man of great culture and intellectual attainments, he would have brought his many gifts and distinction to the task. He had served with the United States Army, been a law clerk to the unflamboyant Supreme Court Justice Tom C. Clark, then practiced law in the corporate and financial fields. He could commend himself to those who prized solid background. At the same time, he had spent years as general counsel of the Illinois division of the American Civil Liberties Union, for whom he had argued the famous *Escobedo* case, forerunner of *Miranda*,[2] before the Supreme Court. He had played leading roles in other committees and organizations devoted to civil rights and, by any test — insight, resourcefulness, training, temperament, and devotion — was qualified to head the Bill of Rights Committee of the Sixth Illinois Constitutional Convention. He had waged a brilliant campaign for election as a delegate and had bearded the secretary of state, the legendary Paul Powell, in a famous law suit concerning electoral practices. By a

[2] *Escobedo* v. *Illinois*, 378 U.S. 478 (1964); and *Miranda* v. *Arizona*, 384 U.S. 436 (1966), respectively.

kind of perversity, some of these very qualities made many respectable persons fear Weisberg. Some later confessed that there were conservatives who at the beginning thought Weisberg and Gertz the most dangerous persons at the convention, to be equally feared. For these and many other reasons, Weisberg and I were natural allies. We did not flatter each other. Indeed, we did not hesitate to be critical; he, perhaps, more so than I. Increasingly, all grew to admire this soft-spoken human dynamo who did not wear his heart on his sleeve, but whose views were never mistaken or ignored. He was of inestimable value to the committee, its chairman, and the convention.

Others thought that the gray-haired, courtly, conservative, informed and unflappable lawyer and businessman of Moline, Lewis D. Wilson, would make an ideal chairman of the committee and keep it out of the grips of the radicals. He was the retired general counsel and vice-president of John Deere and Company, the largest employer in the state, a one-time director and vice-president of the Illinois State Chamber of Commerce, a long-time trustee of the Illinois Taxpayers Federation, on the Board of Governors of the United Republican Fund of Illinois, an active participant in the Goldwater presidential campaign; he had all of the respectable credentials and was a man of substance and charm. He could preside competently, and clearly would not permit extremists to run things in so important an area. But just as some welcomed these qualities of stability, others feared that the committee would not take wings under his direction; that, in short, a more dedicated devotee of individual rights was needed at the helm. Increasingly, I learned to count on Wilson for counsel and support. He was helpful and fair when some supposedly in my corner were neither.

Strange to say, another member of the committee, Mrs. Virginia Macdonald of Arlington Heights, this one an involuntary member, became one of my staunchest personal supporters, even when her votes were cast against my viewpoint. She was a Texan by birth, the daughter of a woman who cherished the literary arts, highly articulate, a devoted Episcopalian, long active in the leadership of the Republican party as committeewoman, county chairwoman, and first vice-president of the Illinois Federation of Republican Women. She had been one of the leaders in the last campaign of Senator

Dirksen. It was assumed by many of the more conservative delegates that she would, naturally, help to contain Gertz, Raby, and Weisberg. They were astounded to find that she made up her own mind and was governed by principles rather than politics. She was a confidante of the promising young organization Democrats, Richard M. Daley, son of the mayor, and his pal Michael Madigan. I was often grateful that, despite her disappointment that she had not been named to one of the three committees of her choice, she did not insist that President Witwer transfer her. Later she grew to cherish her unwanted association with the Bill of Rights Committee, and was one of its great defenders.

When asked to designate our choices, only four members of our committee — Victor Arrigo, Father Lawlor, Bernard Weisberg, and myself — had named the Bill of Rights Committee as first choice. Only two other delegates — Miss Odas Nicholson and William Jaskula — had said that ours was their prime choice, but they had been given other assignments. One other delegate, Thomas Kelleghan, had said that the Bill of Rights Committee was his second choice, and another, Albert Raby, had named it as his third. Thus the committee consisted largely of men and one woman who had not asked to be on it — James Kemp, as vice-chairman, John Dvorak, William Fennoy, Jr., Leonard Foster, Matthew Hutmacher, Arthur Lennon, Virginia Macdonald, Roy Pechous, and Lewis Wilson, these nine in addition to those six who had requested appointment.

It was not that President Witwer lacked potential willing members of the committee. In addition to those already mentioned, delegates Brown, Butler, Kinney, Pughsley, Willer, Downen, Linn, Netch, Patch, Wenum, and Ronald Smith would have been glad to serve, with varying degrees of enthusiasm. But Witwer had in mind the concept of committee balance — political, ideological, geographical, racial; and I sometimes think that subconsciously he wanted to surround the controversial chairman with such a variety of strong-willed persons who disapproved of him that he would be incapable of carving the bill of rights in his own image.

In the end, there were seven Catholics, six Protestants, and two Jews on the committee; four blacks and eleven whites; one woman and fourteen men; seven from Chicago, five from the suburbs, and three Downstaters; six Republicans, five Democrats (including the unpredictable Leonard Foster), three Independent Democrats, and one Independent (Father Lawlor) who was *sui generis;* ten lawyers, one priest, one housewife, one politician, and one teacher; of the lawyers, six had been, or were, connected with governmental agencies, chiefly in prosecution, and two including the chairman were known for defense work, and one, Kelleghan, was on both sides.

There is a more realistic way of profiling the committee. Three (Gertz, Raby, and Weisberg) were the most liberal of the group; four (Kemp, Foster, Wilson, and Mrs. Macdonald) were a sort of swing group, going from liberal to moderate and sometimes conservative; four (Arrigo, Dvorak, Fennoy, and Pechous) were moderates capable, like the others, of going in unexpected directions; and the remaining four (Hutmacher, Lennon, Kelleghan, and Father Lawlor) were almost invariably conservative.

The most liberal bloc were Chicagoans, Independent, two Jewish, and one black. The swing group was evenly divided between blacks and whites, Democrats and Republicans; two were from Chicago, one the suburbs, and one Downstate; it included the one woman of the committee. The moderates consisted of three Democrats and one Republican; two suburban, one Downstate, and two Chicagoans; one black, three white; two Catholic, two Protestant. The conservatives were Republicans, except for the Independent Lawlor; one Downstater, two suburban, and one Chicagoan; all four were Catholics.

Ethnically, there were Irish, Scotch-Irish, English, Italian, Bohemian, German, Jewish, and black members.

Above and beyond all else, they were personalities — diverse, strong, wilful, inquisitive, suspicious, amiable, acrimonious, all too human. Would they be able to work in harness, or would they run off in every direction, and be incapable of performing their assigned task as a team?

James H. Kemp, the vice-chairman of the committee, was very strong-willed, articulate in some respects, and an unfathomable man. I never could feel that he was completely in my corner. I had reason to feel that we ought to be close. We had shared several extremely interesting experiences before the convention had even begun. He had been a member of the Illinois Fair Employment Practices Commission from its outset, and I had been one of those most responsible for the passage of the law creating the commission. I had served without compensation as special counsel for the commission in connection with the famous *Motorola* case,[3] which challenged the validity of the statute and sought to impose upon the commission requirements that might block true non-discrimination. The commission had not been confident that the attorney general, its statutory counsel, was wholly on its side. It had wanted me to act as special counsel in the case and I had agreed to do so. Apparently, Kemp did not regard these things as sufficient reason for showing special courtesy to me. He could be abrupt, unkind, and sometimes, I thought, unfair. I think his occasionally dubious attitude arose out of the initial confrontation between himself, as leader of the black delegates, and Witwer, the convention president. Kemp felt that at least one black, and probably more than one, should be chairman of one of the substantive committees. When, in private conference, Witwer was confronted with this demand, he responded that the black delegates were all Democrats, and with one exception, regular Cook County Democrats, and that therefore the Democrats should surrender at least one chairmanship to the blacks. This they refused to do. Thereupon Kemp attacked Witwer, a long-time board member of the Chicago Urban League, as a racist. The atmosphere was tense indeed during the course of Kemp's bitter address to the convention. He capped it with a resignation from the post of vice-chairman of the Bill of Rights Committee, to which Witwer had assigned him. This last move took the other blacks by surprise. In the end, Kemp reconsidered and remained as vice-chairman of my committee. I went to great lengths to placate and humor him at all times. Occasionally he responded; sometimes he did not.

When later there was the notorious row with Leonard Foster, the self-appointed secretary of my committee, Kemp told me not to take Foster back as secretary: that he would, as he phrased it, chop off my head if I retreated. Taking me completely by surprise, he himself then proposed that Foster come back as secretary. I never quarreled with Kemp as to this point and indeed never said any-

[3] *Motorola v. Fair Employment Practices Commission,* 34 Ill. 2d 266 (1966).

thing to him about it, but I remembered it, not out of vindictiveness, but self-protection. I made a mental note never to depend unduly upon my bright, sometimes amiable vice-chairman.

Most of the time during the committee sessions, but not on the floor of the convention, Kemp and I were in the same corner so far as votes were concerned. On the floor of the convention we battled over judicial selection. The clerk of the convention told me later that the most eloquent speeches made during the course of the debate on the judiciary were by Kemp, Thomas Hunter, and myself. I made it a point, in answering Kemp's highly charged attack upon the merit selection of judges, to refer to my long battle against discrimination and for the brotherhood of man, and in as reasonable tone as possible I gave the arguments for a non-elective judiciary. It was not until weeks later that Kemp chose to reply to my argument on the floor of the convention.

This was typical of the emotional twists and turns in the committee and on the floor of the convention with respect to civil rights matters. Kemp and Hunter had opposed merit selection as a fraudulent device to keep blacks and other minority representatives off the bench. I was notoriously opposed to all forms of racism. I did not have to defend myself on that score. I, therefore, expected and generally received full support from Kemp and other blacks on matters relating to non-discrimination.

There were amazing differences between two of the most highly cultured and intellectual members of the committee — Victor A. Arrigo and Leonard N. Foster. Both Chicagoans and Democrats, supposedly organization men, they were so far apart as to be like planets traveling in distinct orbits. Arrigo, born in Sicily, was yet an American from birth. While Foster sometimes gave the impression of running from his heritage, Arrigo never wavered in his love of all things Italian. He knew everything about the history, the personalities, the arts, the lore, the aspirations, the frustrations of his people, and was their staunchest and most eloquent defender. Woe betide anyone who affronted the Italians in Arrigo's presence. He was the recipient of many awards for distinction in his fields of interest. He was soldier, prosecutor, and legislator (he and Paul Elward were the only two members of the General Assembly who had been elected as delegates). Next to his love for things Italian and artistic, he cherished the legislature and was quick to lecture us on the virtues of that body. One almost saw the Roman toga on Arrigo as he spoke.

Foster, a black, was that member most impatient of and least impressed by Arrigo. Foster was not very patient of anybody, for that matter, and he lacked admiration for those around him. He did have great self-esteem, and this was often justified. Offensive although he may have been, he had singular gifts, evidenced by degrees in psychology, sociology, music, and law. The son of a long-time leader of the Chicago Urban League, whom I had known rather well, he had been brought up in a so-called white North Shore suburb and was unreconciled to the ways of bigots. In many respects, he was closer to the white men and women of the convention than the blacks, who seemed to have a great antipathy to him. He seemed to be in emotional turmoil much of the time, and it was difficult to have a sustained good relationship with him, although he was one of the most eager and useful members of the committee. There were weeks when I felt more sorely tried by him than by anyone else. I endeavored to get rid of my adverse feelings and, after a time and in a fashion, I succeeded. He was indubitably bright, filled with ideas, and often eloquent if biting. Nobody in the convention could ignore him, whether or not they nursed wounds inflicted by him. He and Arrigo gave color to our deliberations.

Arthur T. Lennon was a very shrewd and sometimes cunning attorney from Joliet where he was assistant to the state's attorney and in the private practice of law, as well. Although a Republican, he was often aligned with the Cook County Democrats. He was conservative in viewpoint on most issues and ingenious in giving expression to the reasons for every position that he took and those which he opposed. He had a gift for phrasing amendments that could take the life out of anything which he opposed or could change its meaning. The classical example of his skill, as we shall see, related to the due process section of the bill of rights. His insertion of the words "including the unborn" led to a memorable hassle in the committee and on the floor of the convention, which will be dealt with at length in the course of this narrative.

Lennon seemed to take joy in transforming the ill-considered notions of others in his camp. He would take a poorly expressed proposal of Father Lawlor and give it dimensions. This was true in connection with the due process clause and in other areas.

Purporting to be in favor of non-discrimination, he proposed an extension of the provision with respect to non-discrimination in employment and property that would have gone so far as to make it unlikely that the section could receive a majority vote on the floor of the convention. His substitution called for non-discrimination in every area, including country clubs.

Even when I most differed with Lennon, I often enjoyed being with him. He had a considerable capacity for conversation and what goes with it in cocktail lounges. Early in the convention, he made me very happy by declaring that he hoped he would be on the Bill of Rights Committee in his next incarnation and that I would be chairman of the committee. And when the convention was over, he called me up on Christmas Eve to wish me a happy Chanukah and to tell me how much he enjoyed working with me, despite our differences. These things were not said simply in confidence. He was quoted to the same effect during the period of public debate on the approval or disapproval of our document.

Certain of the more conservative members created annoyances and disharmony at times. Lennon kept one on one's mettle. You had to be good to cope with him — resourceful, perceptive, yielding, or unyielding in particular circumstances. Lennon took his work seriously. He produced witnesses, he participated in the debates, he fielded all over the lot.

Father Francis X. Lawlor was at once the simplest and most complex member of the committee. Whenever anyone wanted to indicate the range of personality and viewpoint on the Bill of Rights Committee, he would say that the membership went from Father Lawlor to Al Raby. In neither instance was this really a fair simile. Neither person was completely like the public impression of him. I had first heard of Father Lawlor through my litigation and speech-making on First Amendment rights, particularly in the area of obscenity cases. I remember once debating various aspects of this highly charged subject with my friend, Judge Norman Eiger. Father Lawlor was in the audience, observant, but silent. The debate took place in his bailiwick, the southwest extremity of the city. Father Lawlor was known as one of the most effective leaders of Citizens for Decent Literature. He undoubtedly looked upon me at the time as an unashamed advocate of dirty books and unclean pictures, and I, to be perfectly frank, thought of him as an over-zealous, uncharitable bigot. The impression deepened as Father Lawlor seemed to oppose the Roman Catholic hierarchy in its apparent efforts to integrate the community. When he formed block clubs and was exiled to Oklahoma, I felt that the community was rid of a dangerous influence, although I believed that, priest or not, Father Lawlor had the right to speak out. He then returned to the city, despite the objections of the cardinal and others, and while excluded from his priestly duties, he participated in public affairs and ran for election to the convention as an Independent. He won overwhelmingly. When he was assigned to my committee, I was rather apprehensive as to what that might mean in our discussions and decisions.

On only a few occasions did Father Lawlor and I clash. I felt that he was rather prolix in his way of communicating. Now and then I would have to tell him to shorten his presentations. He would do so sometimes with protest, and sometimes uncomplainingly. Occasionally, I would have to rule him out of order, but I generally desisted. I tried in every way to make him feel that he was being treated properly. I would take walks with him, and invariably I would ask, "Father, have I been fair to you today?" And invariably, he would say, "Yes, Elmer, you have been fair." On one walk he was particularly confiding, saying that he had the reputation of being a racist, but he really was not one. He said he was deeply concerned about the people in his community. They were losing their homes and businesses and schools and churches, and he did not know how to cope with the situation. He thought the block groups would help. He had no antagonism to the blacks, he said. He was not opposed to open occupancy. I felt at the time that he was deeply earnest and I was inclined to believe him. He told me of his youth in Brooklyn, of the period before his entering the seminary when he was employed in a broker's office. His origin was working class and he seemed to have an instinctive feeling for the interests of the poor.

On one notorious occasion, the committee and the convention were convulsed by an exchange between Father Lawlor and myself. We were debating on some issue or other in our committee and

Father Lawlor delivered a long diatribe against the public schools for their manner of teaching sex to the children. He went on to complain that they did not point out that masturbation was wrong. This led to a long and impassioned speech. It went on and on. Finally, I interrupted the good Father, saying: "Father Lawlor, we have no proposition before the committee on the subject of masturbation." It was perhaps not in good taste, but it ended that prolonged discussion.

On one occasion, delegate Martin Tuchow said to me, "I understand that Father Lawlor has a fetus in a bottle on his desk in the committee room and that he is going to make a speech about it in connection with the debate on abortion." I told Tuchow that he was misinformed. Nobody would do such a thing in our committee. Apparently, I was the only one who had not observed the fetus in the bottle on Father Lawlor's desk. And sure enough, he delivered a long address attacking those who would kill the full-formed, unborn child through abortion. He had much material besides, and he eloquently drew a picture of unconscionable surgeons killing a protesting fetus.

I hesitate to write of Thomas C. Kelleghan because we were so far apart ideologically and in personality, and I do not like to give an unsympathetic portrait. I believe you should limn people only in love, and, try as I might, I could not often love Kelleghan. He had read deeply in political science, philosophy, history (we were both members of the Civil War Round Table), and the law. He was a natural conservative, distrustful of the new, which he was inclined to look upon as radical and revolutionary. He had much of the prosecutor in his make up, and could make witnesses before us feel that they were on trial. He cherished old institutions like capital punishment, and like most of us, he had great confidence in the certainties of his convictions. He was less inclined than some of us to concede the good faith of opponents. I think that one reason he resented me, and it was probably a good reason, was that I had once filed a suit against him for a client. I later stepped out of the matter, but the animosity remained. Still, I must confess, Kelleghan could be charming on occasion, especially when near his lovely children and wife, or when the day's business was at an end and we were relaxing together. He was a fighter normally, breathing fire and brimstone, and he made our meetings volcanic.

The greatest contrast to Kelleghan was presented by another member. Albert A. Raby was an enigmatic character, little of him being visible on the surface. Those who had scarcely heard of him thought him a loud character, a rabble rouser; they were surprised, if not shocked, by his quiet demeanor, his poise, gentility, moderation. A profound believer in non-violence — Dr. Martin Luther King, Jr., was his ideal — he was yet a fighter for the rights of his people and all disadvantaged people, and he stood up firmly for every cause dear to him.

A teacher, Raby was organizer of Teachers for Integrated Education. He then became convenor of the Coordinating Council of Community Organizations and co-chairman with Dr. King of the Chicago Freedom Movement, marching fearlessly at the side of Dr. King through white neighborhoods that hated the very thought of a non-segregated society. He suddenly resigned his position and enrolled in the graduate school of history at the University of Chicago, so that he might know the antecedents of the world that he was seeking to remake. Then he became active in Operation Breadbasket with Rev. Jesse Jackson, the dynamic young follower of the sainted King, and his fertile mind began to think of the problems of tenants in a landlord's world. His campaign for election to the constitutional convention was conducted with great skill. He was a highly valued member of the Independents who on the committee included Gertz and Weisberg, and at the convention, Tomei, Cicero, Mrs. Netsch, Mrs. Leahy, Whalen, and Ronald Smith.

For months, Raby and Tomei roomed together, symbols of the spirit of brotherhood that unites the best people of this world. Months later, after the convention was over and we experienced the great tragedy of Tomei's premature death, it was Raby who delivered the very moving eulogy, never to be forgotten by us.

Raby had a great passion for pool and when he played hooky in Springfield, it was to visit a pool hall. On one notable occasion, he beat Minnesota Fats, and Tomei was quick to have the classic event memorialized in a resolution by the convention.

There was high seriousness and much lightness, and Raby was a part of both. On the committee, he often went by instinct, rather than research. A layman in the midst of lawyers, this was a gift to be valued. Weisberg and I found his collaboration indispensable. Sometimes we three stood alone in the voting. Raby would give great pause to his opponents and trouble their spirits. He professed to hold no dogmatic beliefs, but his was a basically religious influence on the committee and wherever delegates gathered. Virginia Macdonald, who sat next to him, was one of his greatest admirers, as she absorbed the depth of his compassion and intelligence.

If I have not written more about the remaining members of the committee, it is not because of any lack of interest in them. They too held my absorbed attention at times, but they did not enter as fully into the work of the committee or my life. Their very qualities gave a certain obscurity to them, surrounded as they were by uninhibited and strong-willed characters who could not be put down.

Matthew A. Hutmacher was every bit as conservative as Kelleghan, Lennon, and Father Lawlor, but he scarcely raised his voice, even when uttering views that were too traditional to be associated with so young a man. Hutmacher once wrote in a book of mine: "To Elmer, a great committee chairman and a great philosopher and human being with whom I often disagreed." That was typical of him: warm and friendly, never overpassionate. On one occasion, when I was in a buoyant mood, after being defeated on some vote or other, he expressed great amazement at how I could bounce back.

"Butch" — one did not think of him so formally as William F. Fennoy, Jr. — was a folk figure in speech, appearance, history, and viewpoints. He was an inseparable associate of Kemp's. They seemed to delight in trading votes and experiences. A teacher, a family man, above all a politician in an area where the blacks counted, he knew where all the bodies lay, including those that could be counted at election time. He was impatient of the technicalities of lawyers and the pretty talk given out by some. He had a great gift for mimicry. When most silent, he was observing, taking note, planning what he would do.

The two young men of Bohemian extraction had more points of difference than similarity: Roy C. Pechous, a Republican, and John E. Dvorak, a Democrat, had both worked for governmental bodies and both aspired to rise in the political world. Pechous was a bachelor, a loner at times, brought up in Father Flanagan's Boys-town. Dvorak was a family man. They seemed in search of causes, people, influences. They would grow as circumstances compelled.

Two members of the committee got an unexpected first-hand lesson in the meaning of some of the provisions of the bill of rights while they were motoring one day in March to the convention on U.S. highway 66. The two, Roy Pechous and one who prefers anonymity, had been connected with law enforcement themselves; Pechous as an assistant state's attorney in Cook County. Pechous claimed that he was verbally abused and that his automobile was unconstitutionally searched and seized by a state trooper who charged him with speeding. Pechous had detected a vibration in a rear wheel and pulled off the road to inspect the car.

"I decided the tire had enough air to reach the next service station and continued on," he said. "I drove only about five hundred yards when Trooper Cushing ordered me to stop."

Then, according to Pechous, the trooper ordered the two from the car and became belligerent when he was told he did not have permission to search the vehicle. The trooper claimed that he observed a brown paper sack on the front seat and asked what it was. Pechous asked what they were accused of, and was told they were under arrest for driving 88 miles per hour in a 70 mile zone. The trooper ordered Pechous to the squad car and the other man to the side of Pechous' car. The trooper looked into the bag and found that it contained many packages of gum!

The trooper said: "I did not look in the glove compartment nor the trunk as they were both locked. I did look under the seat because many persons carrying open bottles of whiskey or guns hide them there."

Pechous commented: "If two citizens know their rights and are subjected to unreasonable search, what must happen to the guy in work clothes who doesn't know his rights when he gets stopped for a traffic ticket?"

The superintendent of state police declared that convention delegates do not "have immunity from arrests as do members of the legislature and he has instructed all uniformed members of the state police to take appropriate enforcement action with delegates as they would with anyone else."

Pechous commented: "I was known as an extremely hard-nosed prosecutor. I looked askance when a defendant suggested police had violated his rights."

It would be interesting to see how the two newly educated men would react to the discussion before the committee on search and seizure!

Very early in the convention, President Witwer talked with me with respect to the choice for legal counsel for the Bill of Rights Committee. He was much impressed by Professor Dallin H. Oaks, then on leave from the University of Chicago Law School where he had lately presided over disciplinary proceedings involving the student sit-ins. He had had a large number of hearings — something like 165, I believe, and had officiated with both firmness and fairness. He was not idle. He had accepted an assignment from the Department of Justice in Washington to work on the problem of the exclusionary rules made necessary by the *Miranda* decisions and other recent pronouncements of the Warren Court. I knew little of Professor Oaks at the moment, but I was soon to learn much about him, and the more I learned, the more I was impressed.

President Witwer, Oaks, and I lunched together, and Oaks carefully explained to us that while he was much interested in our work, he was not in the position to accept employment from the convention, not even on a part-time basis. We were reluctant to accept the negative response. The more I observed, the more impressed I was by him. He had, for example, been Chief Justice Warren's law clerk. Although young enough to be my son, he had a maturity and self-confidence much beyond his years. A devout Mormon who did not smoke and abstained from all stimulating drinks including coffee, he still did not give the impression that he was a bluenose. He laughed heartily over everything and had obvious zest for his work and for all that went on in the world.

He had been active in the 1964 Goldwater campaign for the presidency and was a far more conservative person than myself, but he won my instant and continuous admiration and affection, despite any and all differences. He would tell me whether he agreed or disagreed with me and why. He had a kind of objectivity that one seldom found.

I talked about him with my friend Professor Harry Kalven, Jr., of the University of Chicago Law School. Kalven and I had served together on the Sparling Commission, which had investigated the peace disorders in Chicago in the spring of 1968 and then the Democratic Convention disorders in the summer of that year. We were akin in a basically liberal orientation. Kalven shared my admiration for his colleague Oaks, despite their philosophical differences. I was determined to overcome Oaks's reluctant refusal to take the proffered position. We talked again, this time alone, and in the end Oaks yielded to my persuasion. I think neither of us ever regretted the decision, although occasionally we had slight differences and once or twice more important ones.

He was an extraordinary counsel for any committee. My own feeling was that he was the very best committee counsel at the convention. Although his time was limited and he hoarded it, he seemed to accomplish more in less time than anyone with whom I was acquainted. He spelled out his schedule for us and how much of it he could devote to our work at the convention. He told us of his method of operation; that, for example, he would use several of the students at the University of Chicago Law School as researchers under his supervision and that they would be compensated at a prescribed rate. He set forth a budget to include all of the expenses and his own compensation. Interestingly, not he but the University of Chicago was to be paid for his services because he was being compensated by the university while he was on leave. He had a scrupulous regard for what was right. At the same time, he had an awareness of the psychological aspects of every situation. He seemed to understand the chairman of the committee and every member. Almost without exception, he was able to deal with the diverse personalities without false steps. There was no political maneuvering on his part, no flattery, nothing unworthy of a self-respecting human being. It was simply diplomatic skill and a desire to establish sufficient territory for successful performance of his duties. I often sat back and admired his virtuoso performances.

When I was subjected to what I regarded as unfair reactions by a few members of the committee, Oaks acted as a reconciling force.

He would give shrewd insight as to what motivated some reactions, and often I was able to correct the situation. We were built, it seemed, for working in double harness. Sometimes I had the delightful feeling that Oaks had a kind of respect and affection for me, similar to what I felt for him. Professor Kalven wrote to me early in our association that he was pleased to see that the marriage of Gertz and Oaks was working out so well.

Much later, I inserted these words in the introductory pages of the committee report: "The committee had the invaluable research guidance and general assistance of Professor Dallin H. Oaks: in consideration of Member and Committee Proposals, in the selection and scheduling of witnesses, in the orderly conduct of the Committee's business, and in the drafting of its report." This is a good illustration of how little mere words mean. Oaks's contribution to our work was invaluable. He refrained from influencing our judgment on substantive matters. He felt, quite properly, that it was up to us to make up our own minds with respect to any proposal that came before us and the final contents of the preamble and bill of rights. Subconsciously, I am sure, he tried to influence our judgment on a few matters dear to him such as the elimination of the federally unconstitutional language in the provision as to libel and, more subtly, with respect to the right to bear arms. Oaks himself had the sportsman's view on arms. Bernard Weisberg, even more than I, felt that in spite of himself, Oaks was showing that he did not disapprove of the majority viewpoint which led to what I still regard as an unfortunate provision in the bill of rights.

Every proposal that came before the committee Oaks analyzed for us, sometimes off the cuff at committee meetings, but more often in memoranda, the "L.A.R.A.M.s" that became so famous in the convention. More than a word should be said about these. The cryptic initials meant Legal and Research Advisor's Memoranda. Oaks was, of course, the legal and research advisor. He recruited a group of University of Chicago Law School students to work under his direction. These included James Franczek, Joseph H. Groberg, Randolph N. Jonakait, David Kroot, Peter C. Parnow, and Katherine B. Soffer. Everything was screened and organized by Oaks himself and bore his imprint. There were fifty of these memoranda, comprising a total of 660 pages. A group of them dealt with the committee business — suggested organization for consideration of bill of rights topics, the Chicago hearings (part of the so-called road show, about which more later), classification of member proposals, statements of issues and topics, the status of committee action, drafts of the committee reports on various provisions, and the like. Other memoranda dealt with virtually all of the provisions of the 1870 bill of rights and preamble and with proposed new provisions, such as arms, counsel in civil cases, administrative review, confession of judgment clauses, discrimination, equal protection, garnishment of wages, individual dignity, the concept of ombudsman, poverty. Constitutional and statutory provisions from everywhere were set forth and analyzed. Leading articles by law professors and others were digested or set forth in full. The pros and cons of everything suggested for the committee's consideration was the subject of at least one memorandum or section thereof. Some problems were so persistent and came before us in such varied form that from time to time the initial memorandum was supplemented. Even the less conscientious members of the committee tried to read these memoranda, if they read nothing else, and would discuss them with Oaks and among themselves.

Even so critical a delegate as Paul Elward, a Daley stalwart, was enthusiastic about the memoranda, although he was not on our committee. On one occasion, he made it a point to tell me that a complete set of the memoranda ought to be placed in the legislative library, so that the members of the house and senate could have the benefit of the in-depth consideration that we had given to so many matters. Oaks himself was not quite that enthusiastic about the memoranda. He insisted that the memoranda ought not to be circulated generally; that indeed, they might be regarded as the confidential records of the committee. This was a viewpoint difficult to implement, because the committee members, in their enthusiasm, were likely to show the memoranda to others, as in the case of Elward.

Oaks, so diplomatic and worldly-wise, unwittingly led us into a rather dismaying episode with the press. The communications media were covering the convention in depth and they were particularly concerned with the Bill of Rights Committee, which made so much news. A spokesman for the press asked to see the memoranda.

Patiently, I explained to him the views of Oaks and other reasons for our reluctance to permit the examination of the documents. The response was obvious. The deliberations of the convention and all of its committees were supposed to be out in the open. The rules of the convention so provided. How could we then make an exception of our material? We persisted at least until we could talk over the matter with Oaks. Meanwhile, newspaper articles and editorials appeared, critical of us. At the same time, we were having difficulty with another staff member and we held an executive session of our committee — this against my own better judgment. Vice-chairman Kemp insisted that, despite the convention rules about open meetings, when personnel were involved there was the necessity for private discussion. The press resented this and commented upon it. A humorous aspect of the situation was that my wife, so popular among the committee membership, had left her crocheting material in the committee room and when she returned to get it, I asked her to leave in an almost angry tone, so upset was I by the necessity to have a closed meeting.

As might have been expected, the most controversial committee of the convention had the most controversial administrative assistant, Lawrence R. Miller, invariably called Larry. I was greatly impressed by Miller when I first interviewed him. He seemed the ideal person for the task. He had been a by-line writer for the *Chicago Daily News* and had managed the campaign for a candidate for Congress in a most energetic fashion. He was gregarious, inquisitive, bright, and cynical. He seemed to grasp what was involved in the work of the Bill of Rights Committee. He met with the committee and he told all of us that he was going to make a special project out of becoming acquainted with each member of the committee, so that he would be able to fulfil all of our individual needs.

Despite my liking for him, I soon found myself dissatisfied with the manner in which he was functioning. I expressed myself in unmistakable terms and told him that I would dispense with his services. Then Dallin Oaks brought us together and we became quite cordial again. Thereafter, I sometimes wondered why he had so disturbed me. At the time I was most reconciled to him, other members of the committee, notably Foster and Kelleghan, became increasingly dissatisfied. Foster, a stickler at times for propriety, objected to Miller's coming to the convention floor in his shirt sleeves and with his hair in disarray. Foster felt that Miller did not follow his instructions and indeed thwarted him. Kelleghan felt that Miller was conspiring to present to us only the most liberal viewpoint on all issues.

When it became known that Miller was keeping notes and that he intended to write a book about our committee, I was amused, but Kelleghan and Foster were outraged. They felt that, in good conscience, Miller had to clear the matter with us, and that we ought to see his notes and what he wrote. Politely, but firmly, Miller refused to bend. He said that he would violate no confidences in his book. What he would write would be his own and no one else would control him. It seemed rather amusing to me, if not rather ominous even to seek to question the right of the administrative assistant to the freedom of expression. My feeling was that if Miller was doing his work, what he did on his own time was his own business and not ours. At the very time when others were attacking him, I felt most defensive of him.

If Miller had enemies on the committee, he also had friends, and some of them spoke up for him when on the insistence of the vice-chairman we held an executive session. In the end, even Kelleghan withdrew his charges during our private meeting. When we took a vote, everyone except Foster voted to commend Miller. Then, as I recall, Foster changed his vote to "present." The embroglio ended with an anticlimax. Miller decided that he was going to leave the committee before its work was completed and go into public relations on his own. By coincidence, he became the partner of Mrs. Ann Galloway, the very capable individual to whom we later entrusted our unsuccessful campaign to obtain approval of the separate submission on the abolition of the death penalty.

In the midst of all these carniverous creatures, there was a shy little woman named Juanita R. Gratton, secretary of the committee, or, as Foster called her, our clerk. Juanita seemed to observe everything that went on in our lively meeting room as if in disbelief, as if shrinking from it. Later I learned that she had much admiration, awe even, for many of us, but was simply overwhelmed. She did all that was expected of her in the way of record-keeping, the giving of notices, correspondence, whatever we gave her, working long hours, much of the time under the supervision of Foster, to whom, diplomatically, I surrendered some of my prerogatives, including, often, my private office. Juanita never complained to me, but when I had my main row with Foster, he let it be known that she was going to quit. She never did and I don't really know if she ever had that intention.

There was stacked inside the entrance of the Coe Building in Springfield, used by several committees of the constitutional convention, a pile of heavy table legs, desk arms, and ponderous pieces of wood. Less than a day later some village Royko attached a sign to the material, reading: "Bill of Rights Committee Debate Materials." It remained there for weeks.

Around that time, one of the younger delegates was married. His desk was appropriately bedecked with a shotgun, marked: "Gift from the Bill of Rights Committee."

Other stories about the committee circulated, most of them being characteristic of the more bizarre side of this bitterly divided, highly personal, brilliant and committed group of persons. The one woman on the committee, Virginia Macdonald, was sweet and matronly in the midst of carnage. Sometimes it seemed that only her presence prevented fatalities.

Even the courtly retired corporation counsel, Lewis Wilson, could be biting at moments when he was stung by something or other that he resented.

Yet it was appropriate that there should be this concern over basic issues. Fighting words had given birth to the earliest Bill of Rights, and vigilance was still required to preserve those hard won rights of free men.

The chairman tried to keep a tight rein, even when he himself was the object of attack. He tried to be most fair to those whose views he disagreed with. He would occasionally be most abused as when his close friend on the committee charged him with letting him down, with bad faith.

On the floor of the convention Father Lawlor moved that there be daily prayer. Had he suggested this for the committee, it would have done no good, nor would fasting. These were ravenous crea-

tures at times, intent upon devouring their opponents when the
exigencies of debate required it.

The extensive press coverage of the Bill of Rights Committee
deliberations might be faulted for overstating all that was garish and
extreme, and underplaying the valid and conscientious work of
almost every member of the committee. As long as the reports were
reasonably accurate, I did not much care. My annoyance at some
of the personal barbs was softened by the recollection of what the
one American president whom I could call my friend — Harry S.
Truman — had said in similar circumstances: "If you can't stand
the heat, stay out of the kitchen." As a matter of sober truth, I was
beginning to enjoy the heat and I seemed to thrive on it. There
was a kind of glow in my face as I grew increasingly determined to
confound the critics by coming up in the end with a bill of rights
that would win ready approval.

Even today I recall one newspaper article, more than any other,
with huge delight. It was written by a very young and impious
correspondent of the *Chicago Daily News*. It merits repetition in full
for the true flavor it offers of the committee as it sometimes was.
On May 8, 1970, days before we had filed our report, John Camper
wrote:

> The rock 'em–sock 'em bill of rights committee — already the talk
> of the talk-prone Illinois constitutional convention — had one of
> its wildest afternoons Thursday.
>
> It all started when delegate Bernard Weisberg of Chicago com-
> plained that the committee had reneged on a promise by voting on
> a search and seizure provision that morning in his absence.
>
> In that vote, the committee had changed its earlier ban on eaves-
> dropping devices and agreed to outlaw only "unreasonable" eaves-
> dropping. Weisberg feared the Legislature and courts might decide
> that almost nothing was "unreasonable."
>
> Weisberg moved to reconsider, but was ruled out of order because
> he hadn't voted on the original motion.
>
> "Then I move to reconsider," said delegate Albert A. Raby of
> Chicago.
>
> But first, said chairman Elmer Gertz of Chicago, the committee
> would have to dispose of an amendment to the search and seizure
> article, an amendment to the amendment and a substitute motion.
> All concerned the need for a warrant before any search or seizure.

Delegate Arthur T. Lennon of Joliet said that to expedite matters he was willing to withdraw his motion and proceed directly to a vote on the substitute offered by delegate Lewis D. Wilson of Moline.

"You can't vote on a substitute if there's nothing to substitute it for," said delegate Leonard N. Foster of Chicago. "If Lennon withdraws his motion, then I move it (Lennon's motion)."

The committee then approved the Lennon-Foster amendment, voted down the amendment to the Lennon-Foster amendment and then threw out the Lennon-Foster amendment and approved the Wilson substitution. Then it voted down the Raby-Weisberg motion to reconsider the whole matter.

With this out of the way, the committee settled down to 20 minutes of bickering about when to hold its next meeting.

Lennon moved to continue meeting Thursday evening. Weisberg moved to meet next Tuesday. Gertz moved to meet Friday morning.

Foster said there wouldn't be all this squabbling if everyone were as faithful in committee attendance as he was.

"I haven't missed a committee meeting and I've only been late for two," he said.

Somewhere along the line, delegate Victor A. Arrigo, of Chicago tried to sum everything up by comparing the committee to a tragicomic opera.

"This committee could apply to the Lyric Opera to do 'I Pagliacci,' " he chuckled.

Foster, his face taut with anger, stood up and snapped:

"May I remind Mr. Arrigo that the last words in 'I Pagliacci' are 'La commedia e finita.' "

Translated, that means, "The comedy is over."[4]

Is this not a Dickensian masterpiece?

Earlier, Camper's teammate, the shrewd and sometimes cynical Edward S. Gilbreth, had truthfully said that no committee at the convention had been as "beleaguered" as ours; for the reason that it "faces the most emotionally charged questions that will come before the convention." He listed some of these issues, including: "How to phrase guarantees of basic liberties in a climate of public opinion increasingly suspicious of the right to dissent." He said that I, as

---

[4] John Camper, "Parliamentary maze: Con-Con panel stands pat on softer search-seizure ban," *Chicago Daily News,* May 8, 1970.

chairman, had "tried to reject any attempts to stifle debate on the committee." He observed, with his usual perspicasity: "A few other chairmen, mindful of the disproportionate attention focused on Gertz's committee, hope to get proposals 'eased out' of their committees with a minimum of dissent. This move, if successful, could result in a number of bland committee reports."[5]

[5] Edward S. Gilbreth, "5–day week being urged for Con-Con," *Chicago Daily News,* April 4–5, 1970.

III

The Committee Proceedings

It will be well to consider what came before the committee in the course of its deliberations. First of all, there was the 1870 Illinois Constitution and the earlier constitutions of the state, and there were the federal constitution and the constitutions of the various states. These were the raw materials on which the committee members and the delegates generally were to work. There were those who temperamentally were committed to reaffirming exactly what was in the 1870 constitution. None wanted to retreat from it. Some were willing to consider substantial advances and certain changes of verbiage.

To assist us in our deliberations, there was the Braden and Cohn commentary on the 1870 constitution, the studies put out by the Constitution Research Group, the Model State Constitution, and other similar treatises. Many committee members had come to the convention with pet ideas of their own or thoughts that had been implanted in them by concerned citizens and pressure groups. The machinery for considering these things was both simple and logical, and it worked out exceedingly well. The Bill of Rights Committee made certain additions, but generally it followed the pattern set forth in the rules of the convention. There was a period of time during which all members were free to introduce so-called member proposals, which in the first instance were cleared through the Legislative Reference Bureau, so that, at least superficially, they would be phrased properly. They were then assigned by the convention president to the appropriate committee. The Bill of Rights Committee was one of the first three in volume of business sent to it by the presiding officer, despite the fact that some proposals that properly could have gone to it were sent to other committees.

After a considerable period of time, a deadline was reached for the filing of member proposals. This was briefly extended, and then the time for filing such proposals was at an end. Of course, this did not create a hardship. Every committee member could suggest amendments and new proposals in the deliberations of his committee. Every delegate to the convention could suggest amendments and substitutions from the floor of the convention during the course of debate. This was not a closed convention; indeed, all of the deliberations had to be in the open, with the press and public admitted at all times. Nor was it a closed committee. The reverse was true. The committee valued discussion, differences of opinion, the unexpected.

The Bill of Rights Committee, like all other committees of the convention, had many meetings at which witnesses were heard and often interrogated. There were extended debates. The committee had the assistance of its counsel and others. Ultimately, it came up with its proposals for the preamble and the bill of rights based upon the majority vote of the committee. This was supported by a majority report and, in ten instances, there were minority reports. These things will be dealt with in appropriate detail later.

The convention resolved itself into the committee of the whole for consideration of the proposals of the Bill of Rights Committee as it did in the case of proposals from other committees. There was unlimited debate, unlimited right to amend and substitute, and votes were taken on every amendment, every substitution, and what was left. What befell the committee proposals on each reading will be discussed more fully later. In any event, there was approval on first reading, and what was approved was sent to the Committee on Style and Drafting for language changes, but presumably not for changes in substance. The Committee on Style and Drafting reported back in writing to the convention for second reading consideration. Again, there was unlimited debate and the right to amend and substitute and votes taken, and again approval by the committee of the whole and submission back to the Committee on Style and Drafting.

Finally, the preamble and the bill of rights came back for final vote before the convention in formal fashion in plenary session. There could be no substantive amendments or substitutions without suspension of the rules, which required approval by a majority of the delegates elected. Nonetheless, as we shall see, changes were proposed following suspension of the rules and some changes were in fact made; others were beaten off. In the end, the preamble and bill of rights evolved into the form in which they were submitted to the voters, together with the rest of the constitution and certain so-called separate submissions. Then they became integral parts of the Illinois Constitution of 1970, the separate submission on capital punishment having been defeated.

This process, briefly and categorically described, shows at once the potential for achieving a wise result. The built-in safeguards, the public attention focused upon the deliberations, the desire of each delegate to express himself fully and frankly, the general atmosphere that is part of a constitutional convention, all contributed to a result in which virtually every delegate took pride. On final reading, the bill of rights was approved with only one negative vote and a few abstentions. This indicates, despite all the interim differences, a true consensus. It was achieved only through sweat, dedication, and perhaps even inspiration. This is a story of the achievement and how it was brought about.

There were so many fascinating and significant proposals discussed in committee and in convention, and so many remarkable statements were made, that the full transcript is highly readable and rewarding. The many volumes of wise and witty, foolish and fraudulent statements are indispensable to the interpretation of the various sections, and are well worth reading. And there was the human drama. The 116 delegates were more than the usual representative body. They were extraordinary persons in their devotion to their work, their articulateness, and for other qualities. There are tapes, also, of our committee's discussions, recording almost unbelievable by-plays of personality and principle. Perhaps Larry Miller's manuscript, if it is ever published, will give the flavor of our sessions. Certainly, the press coverage did that in some measure. Here I will try to give the essence only of what went on, the spirit, rather than the details. This narrative does not profess to be the complete story of what we said and did on our lively committee. I tell enough, I hope, to make the interim and final results understandable. I hope that some of the excitement remains, despite the necessary scholarly scaffolding. By summarizing our committee reports in a later chapter, I hope I will tie everything together and make it sufficiently clear.

The committee was very desirous that it not act in haste and that anything that it did might be reconsidered before there was a final disposition of any proposal. The committee felt that the usual parliamentary rule giving the right to ask for reconsideration only to those who had voted on the prevailing side was too stringent. It was decided, unanimously as I recall, that within seven days of any action of the committee on any proposal submitted to it, any member of the committee, regardless as to how he had voted initially, would have the right to request a reconsideration of the matter, that is, more discussion and a second vote. True, this led to a lot of maneuvering by committee members and delegates generally. In some instances the initial vote was possibly sounder than the second and final vote, but nobody could justly complain that the Bill of Rights Committee did not afford full opportunity for consideration and reconsideration. In that respect, I believe, its practice was more fair and flexible than that of any other committee. Not everyone understood the seven-day rule and this included the reporters, who were around every day. Every once in a while, there would be a question as to whether or not there had been a second vote, thus precluding further reconsideration. In one dramatic instance, I first ruled that a revote was in order, and then when I analyzed the situation further, I concluded that it was no longer in order. Since my ruling affected a proposal presented by Father Lawlor, I was afraid that there might be repercussions, but to my delight, my ruling was accepted and nobody appealed from it.

Almost everyone on the committee seemed to have a favorite proposal, and the more grasping or committed had more than one subject of consuming interest. Fennoy, because he had been the victim himself of the absence of an operative provision to prevent prolonged detention without a court hearing, fought for the section on preliminary hearings, although he did not quite grasp what it entailed. Instinctively, he was able to reject anything that imperiled his pet provision. Arrigo was determined to bring about a provision on individual dignity, and woe betide anyone who stood in his way. Kemp, victimized by both discrimination and wiretaps, wanted to ban both, and allied himself, however uncertainly, with those who could help him in this quest. Raby, conscious of those on the lower rungs of the social ladder, felt that there ought to be a pronouncement that all persons are entitled to the basic necessities of life. Weisberg did not want anyone to be committed to jail, whether through bail or fine, simply because he was poor. Father Lawlor was determined to fight for or against proposals as they affected his Catholic faith. Kelleghan was not so much for things as against them. He was for an unchanged constitution and against innovation, a mortal sin in his eyes. Lennon and Hutmacher, temperamentally conservative, both distrusted change; Lennon delighted in performing verbal operations on the ideas of others, and Hutmacher was for a gun provision, but little else that was new either in language or substance. I suppose that I cherished First Amendment freedoms more than all else and was alert to dangers in this area. A few had no hangups.

With strong willed men of varying convictions, there were bound to be invective and abuse, and criticism that sometimes transcended the permissible. Something in my nature enabled me to tolerate the worst, whether it was directed against me or others. When I am criticized, I may feel at first that it is unjust; then instinctively I ask myself if there is a kernel, or more, of truth in the criticism. This often saves me from responding too violently.

Various subcommittees took the initiative in performing tasks that would ease the work of the full committee. Perhaps the most important of these was the subcommittee on scheduling, headed by Vice-chairman James Kemp and including two such diverse members as Bernard Weisberg and Thomas Kelleghan. It put in a good deal of effort, largely in collaboration with Dallin Oaks and Larry Miller, and often in association with me. The theory was that if we planned our efforts, assigning days and hours for each subject, we would hear witnesses, including experts, on all the problems that confronted us and perform our duties in a truly conscientious fashion. It was easy enough to lay out a schedule and, with ideas from the entire membership, to come up with the best persons to express each viewpoint. It was a different matter actually to get the proposed witnesses to come down to Springfield at the scheduled times. Larry Miller was in charge of this effort. By correspondence, but mostly by telephone, he made contacts and lined up people for each day. We had the problem of conflicts with the plenary sessions of the convention. I pleaded with President Witwer to set aside days, or portions of days, when the convention would not be in session, so that the committees, and particularly ours, could function. Once or twice this was done, and we all profited from it. There were occasions when witnesses came down and we could not hear them because the convention was in session, and according to the rules no committee was supposed to meet at such times. Some witnesses got discouraged, and did not remain or return.

I cautioned Miller to be circumspect in getting all viewpoints represented, but there were complaints, particularly by Kelleghan, that Miller was inviting only the A.C.L.U. kind of witness. When the debate became bitter, I urged Kelleghan and others to bring in any witnesses they chose to have. Father Lawlor, availing himself of the invitation, brought in a very belligerent and articulate witness against abortions. William Fennoy brought in witnesses in favor of preliminary hearings for persons accused of felonies, and this led to witnesses on the other side. Some who could not come in sent very helpful letters, at the urging, in several instances as I recall, of Hutmacher and Wilson. Miller had been asked to bring in representatives from the state's attorney's office of Cook County. He tried, he insisted, unsuccessfully. Yet State's Attorney Edward Hanrahan complained to Arrigo that he had not been invited. This led to almost contemptuous questioning of Miller and sometimes of the chairman. It was much easier to complain and accuse than to do anything about it in the way of personally correcting the situation. As a matter of fact, even before the dispute over omissions, as I recall, some members of the committee, including Kemp and Kelleghan, wanted to call off the further hearing of witnesses. I had to plead to permit those already invited to appear if only as a simple act of courtesy, if not for more important reasons.

Yet there was a time early in the convention when all the committee members wanted to hear almost literally everyone. Father Lawlor, for one, suggested that we ought to prepare a complete list of civic and neighborhood organizations with varying viewpoints and invite all of them to appear before us. I asked Virginia Mac-donald to chair a subcommittee for this purpose and had Arrigo, Father Lawlor, and Raby work with her. Enlisting the aid of Peter Pappas, husband of delegate Mary Pappas and a special assistant to the secretary of state, they strove to get a complete list of not-for-profit, public interest corporations. The office of the secretary of state assigned a task force to the job and came up with a compilation that ran into several thick volumes. We looked at the thousands of names in dismay and scarcely utilized the list. But we were grateful and effusively thanked all who had worked so well. Then, when our place of meeting changed from one building to another and our materials were moved, the vast list disappeared. Accusations were made, suspicions were scarcely allayed, until one day, near the end of the convention, the volumes were rediscovered. At that point, we thoughtfully re-presented them to the secretary of state.

We gave much thought to the witnesses we ought to induce to appear before us. Should all public officials be invited, the officers or executive directors of interracial organizations, ordinary citizens, experts, the well known? I thought, for example, of inviting former Justice Arthur J. Goldberg. I knew and respected him, and he had endorsed my candidacy for delegate to the convention; he was from Illinois and he was deeply concerned about the bill of rights. He could not appear at the time, but suggested an invitation to former Chief Justice Warren, whom he thought would appear if we explained why we needed him. I was intrigued by the idea; then I decided that if Warren appeared, it should be before the full convention and that an invitation to him might needlessly stir some sensitive souls. We could advocate the high principles of the great chief justice without arousing unnecessary antagonisms. On reflection, I am not sure that this was a wise decision. We invited both the former Attorney General Ramsey Clark, and the director of the F.B.I., J. Edgar Hoover; neither could attend. The less cele-brated witnesses had knowledge in the areas with which we were con-cerned, and they probably did as well as the big-named personalities.

When we issued a general invitation, we could never tell who would accept it. Thus in Chicago a leading member of the Commu-nist party testified. We received him politely; he had his say and departed; and the world did not come to an end. I do not recall that he was especially helpful.

Our great enemy was verbosity, our own and that of witnesses. We tried to limit all speeches, but more than once individual members and witnesses would protest when reminded of time limitations.

Father Lawlor was deeply concerned about obscenity. Whenever we talked about the subject, he seemed to have the chairman of the committee in mind. The subject of obscenity came to a head when Emmett Dedmon, editorial director of the Field newspapers in Chicago, testified before our committee for complete acceptance — no surprise there! — of the concept of full freedom of expression. Dedmon said that children should be protected against pornography, but that he did not see how it could be covered in the constitution. Father Lawlor was not satisfied. He criticized the press, declaring that the extreme candor with which it covered sensational news was a threat to public morality.

"Don't newspapers have a responsibility to provide us with leadership for patriotism, good moral standards, and respect for each other?" he demanded of Dedmon.

Dedmon, in as reasonable a tone as he could muster, defended the press, maintaining that there was much less sensationalism than in the previous generation. Father Lawlor would not be placated.

Then, after Dedmon's testimony, David Goldberger, staff counsel for the American Civil Liberties Union, told us that the new constitution should not deal with obscenity. "It's our position," he said, "that so-called obscenity is socially harmless and only offends sensitivity. You shouldn't legislate against anything unless it's proved harmful."

That was all Father Lawlor needed to hear. He debated the matter with Goldberger, who was polite but unyielding. Obscenity, Father Lawlor declared was "eating away at the soul of America." He said that "stag shows, stag films and almost anything goes" in Chicago, because of the A.C.L.U. which volunteered its services to "defend these deranged minds" in their assault upon community standards.

It was about that time that Father Lawlor insisted that Edward Clancy, general counsel of Citizens for Decent Literature, be invited to testify before us on the subject of obscenity. I had encountered Clancy in litigation involving a film in Cincinnati, the home base of the founder of Clancy's organization, Charles Keating, who had instigated the prosecution. I welcomed the opportunity to confront Clancy again and suggested to Father Lawlor that he invite Clancy for a designated date. There was some question as to the length of his appearance. As I recall, Father Lawlor suggested an extraordinarily long time, almost as if the fate of the convention depended on Clancy's words. With misgivings, I told Father Lawlor to proceed with the arrangements. But Clancy never did show up. I next saw him more than a year later when he and I argued a case before the Ohio Supreme Court. By that time our convention had concluded its business without any clause on obscenity.

Most members of the committee were willing to work as many days and as long hours as required. Some were willing to work long hours, but only three days per week; they had their law practices, their trade union duties, other necessary tasks to perform. The convention rules gave the committee chairmen the right to fix the times of committee meetings and the agenda. But I was content to go along with the minority who were not willing to devote their full time to our work. I felt that within a few days each week we crowded in more actual work than the other committees, for we worked long hours and had our scheduling extremely well organized. There came a time, however, when it became necessary to insist upon meetings on one or more additional days each week; the schedule of the convention demanded it. I sought unsuccessfully to obtain voluntary compliance with a new work program. There was resistance. I then announced that I felt it my duty to assert the authority given me under the rules. There were loud protests. On one occasion when I called a meeting, the group of rebels failed to show up and there was no quorum. In the end, the committee met as often as necessary and we finished our work somewhat later than I had hoped, but ahead of other major committees.

I recalled my meeting with the director of the Better Government Association during the course of the campaign for election of convention delegates. "We know your qualifications," he said, "but will you really give the convention all the time that it requires?" I assured him that I would. He wanted me to spell out what I intended to do about my busy law practice. I told him and he was satisfied. This personal experience makes me believe that perhaps every constitutional convention delegate and, indeed, every public official ought to be required to pledge that he will devote all of his time to his public responsibilites, to the exclusion of all else. Such a requirement would have given more repose to our deliberations.

It was clear that the constitutional convention would have to come up with some sort of environmental bill of rights. Suddenly, demands were arising everywhere from all sorts of people — including some not usually concerned about matters of public interest — that something drastic be done about the pollution of our planet. There were many who seemed to feel that we were in a crisis in which survival was at stake, and they proposed every wise and foolish idea imaginable to cope with the situation. It was expected that the popular excitement would be translated into many member proposals, which would be sent by President Witwer to the Bill of Rights Committee; for the right to a decent environment was equated with such basic American rights as freedom of expression, religious freedom, protection against unreasonable searches and seizures, and the like. I was prepared to give the subject its due, especially since my one-woman Gallup pollster, my wife, assured me that no matter was of more immediate interest to the people — this even before I had realized the intensity of the concern.

Then one day I was waited upon by the chairman and vice-chairman of the General Government Committee, Thomas Mc-Cracken and Robert Canfield. "Your committee has more to do than time permits," they said to me, in effect. "Let our committee handle the subject of environment." Being in a benevolent mood, I acceded; besides, I knew that with dynamic Mary Lee Leahy on the General Government Committee, something good was bound to be proposed by that brightest and most resourceful and persistent of young women. It was! I am not sure that she could have done as well with my committee.

Still, our committee heard a number of witnesses on the subject in Springfield, our home base, and in Waukegan and Chicago, when we took to the road. In Waukegan, State Representative Daniel M. Pierce urged that we adopt an "environmental bill of rights." The bill, he said, would guarantee everyone in Illinois the rights to breathe clean air, drink pure water, avoid pesticide poisoning, and in general live in a healthy environment. Jeffrey D. Diver, an aspirant for the state senate, seconded Representative Pierce's proposal. He urged that there be only one state agency to control and direct the efforts. Robert W. Layer, Jr., declared the quality of American life was deteriorating because of our ecological mistakes. At this point our secretary, Leonard Foster, asserted that man himself was the greatest pollutant; that before long there would be wall-to-wall people. So it went. What was the answer? Surely not the constitutionalizing of castration, as some seemed to hint at. I won't soon forget the rage of Father Lawlor and Kelleghan when several scientists and students from the University of Illinois, who appeared before us one night in Springfield, urged the limitation of population as the one path to a less crowded and less polluted society. Others were less drastic in their environmental nostrums. It was a subject that lent itself to zealots, all of whom seemed to find their way to our committee.

The Bill of Rights Committee met in Waukegan on February 11, 1970, as part of the constitutional "road show," as some called it not unkindly. Various committees met in different communities of the state and single members of each committee made up panels in yet other communities. The convention was resolved to give all citizens the opportunity to present evidence without having to leave their communities. So far as we know, this was the first time any constitutional convention had embarked upon such a program. So successful was it that other multi-committee panels, including Bill of Rights Committee members, went into yet other cities of the state at a later date. We were able to judge at least partially the extent to which certain proposals and problems interested some communities more than others; and we found that some problems aroused interest no matter where we traveled.

In Waukegan, abortion was a subject of special interest, but there were other excitement-provoking issues as well: equal rights, public aid for private schools, legislation to arm pollution fighters. We spent over five hours listening to over fifty witnesses, some representing organizations, others on their own. "We are here to learn what's on your mind," I said, "not to cross-examine." I was thinking of avoiding the kinds of embarrassment sometimes engendered by the practices of a few members. Father Lawlor would not be contained, and I had to cut short his quarreling with witnesses at least twice when abortion was under discussion. Jeffrey Diver, speaking on various matters, at one point advocated "the right of parents to determine, limit or control the number of their children by means of contraception, abortion, or by voluntary sterilization. That right," he said, "should not be abridged by the state."

Father Lawlor asked: "Would you be willing to make the rights of parents to limit the size of their families retroactive? When a child becomes a pest could his parents kill him?"

Of course Diver readily replied: "No."

At this time Arrigo asked: "If the doctors can't agree, how can the average layman determine if a fetus is living? Are you aware that some of our most magnificent minds have belonged to illegitimate children? We would have lost those great minds if abortion had been permitted."

Mrs. Ruth Zaugg, formerly with a family service organization, seconded by Mrs. Susan McCutchen, of Illinois Citizens for the Medical Control of Abortion, advocated the abolition of abortion laws, saying that a woman has a basic right to decide whether or not to bear a child, that a physician should not be hampered professionally, and that every child brought into the world should be wanted. Both women were filled with information on their subject and poured it forth in full volume while Father Lawlor and Arrigo seemed at times to writhe.

Foster asked Mrs. Zaugg if she would still favor liberalized abortion laws if good birth control methods were available. "Yes," she replied. Father Lawlor espoused the right of the unborn child to live. So the give and take went as a sort of dress rehearsal for what we would hear in Chicago the next day and when we returned to Springfield. Earlier in the day at a luncheon sponsored by the publisher of the *Waukegan News-Sun,* I had said semi-humorously: "We've only had two controversial proposals so far — to abolish the state of Illinois and to abolish the city of Chicago." We had a fistful of controversy that day and even more later.

Professor Franklin Zimring, consultant to the National Commission on Causes and Prevention of Violence, testified before us, urging that we say nothing in the constitution as to any right to bear arms. The matter should be left to the legislature, he said. Father Lawlor interjected that there was a "psychological security" in having a handgun to protect one's home. And what if a big ruffian weighing a couple of hundred pounds sought to rape a little woman? Would she not find protection in a gun?

Robert Kukla, legislative chairman of the Illinois Rifle Association, disagreed with Prof. Zimring. "I care very deeply about the right of the responsible individual to decide for himself if he wants to have a firearm for any legitimate purpose," he said.

Such testimony prompted the *Chicago Sun-Times* and other newspapers to editorialize against a constitutional provision on any right to arms. It accused the National Rifle Association of being "up to its old lobbying tricks." Yet the debate continued, the progun forces gaining unexpected strength without the opponents being aware of it.

Father Lawlor continued to advocate guns as a means of self-defense. "This is a right that I have from God," he said. On this, as well as other issues, he often expressed the conviction that he was doing God's work.

Raby responded, expressing his pacifist faith to the gentleman of the cloth. "As Martin Luther King said, 'an eye for an eye' leaves both persons blind," he said in his soft spoken, simple manner that was winning friends for him in the convention, but not on this issue.

Even Elbert Smith, so genial, so good-hearted, so wise on so many issues, felt compelled to appear before us in defense of the citizen's right to arms. Smith was the vice-president of the convention regularly assigned to our committee.

"The gun on the farm is just about like the coffeepot," Smith said. Raby, Weisberg, and I did not appreciate this, but we stood alone on the committee. Smith tried to smooth our feelings. "There are no near neighbors, and police protection is far away."

Henry Hendren, a delegate from the southern part of the state, spoke with an inflection that momentarily puzzled me, if not others on the committee. He seemed to be talking about "rabbit skunks" and the need for protection against them, when I suddenly realized he was talking about "rabid skunks," snakes, and other menaces in rural areas including, I suppose, strangers.

When Weisberg suggested that we ought to get an opinion from the corporation counsel of Chicago as to that city's viewpoint, Foster declared that he could assert, on the authority of the corporation counsel, that he was not opposed to the proposed section.

"Five years ago," said Weisberg, "no one would have thought about putting such language in the state's charter. It's spawned by anxiety, tension, social unrest, and disorder, and curiously, all of the law and order people are for it."

Arrigo proclaimed his desire to bridge the gap between Chicago and Downstate. His great "compromise" was the insertion of a proviso making the right to arms subject to the police power.

The gun provision debate was the most bitter of any that had divided the Bill of Rights Committee and the vote on it, the first taken by any committee, shocked the leadership of the convention, the press, civic groups, almost everyone except the delegates. The temptation is great to give all of the details — at least the highlights — of the debate.

Excitement mounted almost by the minute after the initial vote in favor of the right to arms provision. The subject in itself was explosive, and doubly so by reason of being the very first section on which any committee had voted. Did it auger an orientation to the right on the part of the committee and perhaps of the convention? Did it mean that the chairman had no control whatsoever of the committee? Would it be a runaway body? Was there any secret deal between the Chicago Democrats and Downstate? If so, what was the *quid pro quo?* Was there any chance of a reversal in committee or by the convention? These and other questions were immediately raised. The press, radio, and television people in Springfield, Chicago, and throughout the state interviewed the chairman and virtually all of the members of the committee. The officers and staff of the convention and many individual delegates were aroused and made inquiry, open and covert. Civic organizations, law enforcement agencies, it seemed almost everyone was involved in one way or the other in the excitement. No one was more concerned than President Witwer. He feared it could wreck the convention, and as the flood of angry editorials began to appear, this was not an unreasonable expectation. He telephoned me several times during that weekend; we met for hours on Saturday and planned our strategy. He would call every member of the committee and others; I would call some also. We would use every legitimate argument to change the result. It was fortunate, we agreed, that our committee had a second vote rule that did not depend upon a motion to reconsider by one who had been on the prevailing side. We checked back with each other before the next regular session of the convention. We seemed to have the votes to reverse the result, but we kept our fingers crossed. Those who changed their minds once could change again. We had no one on our side until the votes were actually counted. Who knew who was active on the other side? The rifle associations, downstate delegates, all sorts of determined and resourceful people would be working against us.

I freely admit that it is difficult for me to understand the emotions of the gun advocates. I am not a sportsman. I share Bernard Shaw's view that it is wrong to kill for sport or indeed for any reason. Truth to tell, I am frightened even of unloaded guns; and I carry the memory through many years of one of my brothers who hovered between life and death for days when he was shot by a hold-up man in his place of business. His eyes had wandered to a nearby gun, and by reflex action the hopped-up robber had shot him. He had survived only by a miracle. I knew that when guns are around they will be used. I did not want them around. I awaited the re-vote with great anxiety.

Encouraged by the reports from President Witwer as to his conversations with some of the members of my committee, I began to feel more hopeful of reversing the vote on guns. "I get the feeling, partly in view of press coverage," I told those who inquired, "there will be reconsideration of this matter. Committee members were actually mesmerized by some of the witnesses." Grasping at straws, I remarked that in some respects the vote was a healthy thing. "It shows I'm no despot." I should have said, perhaps, that there were fifteen despots on the committee, and not just the chairman.

There were reports that John Dvorak had changed his mind. He was quoted as saying: "I've reconsidered. . . . The language might be misinterpreted to prohibit Chicago from regulating handguns." There were other reports that the vice-chairman, Kemp, absent when the first vote was taken, would be a restraining influence when next we voted. Mrs. Macdonald's suburban territory was believed to be distressed by her vote, and that she might change it. Mrs. Macdonald was one of the delegates most attuned to public opinion. She frequently was in communication with the press and civic and political organizations.

The press in various parts of the state joined in the protest against our first vote. Among others, the newspaper in East St. Louis editorialized against the gun provision. Perhaps Fennoy from that territory would heed the press of his area. The Chicago Bar Association, through its very vigorous president Frank Greenberg, issued a strong statement against our gun provision. Raby and I hastened to cheer Mr. Greenberg. Would any of our Chicago members do likewise? Lewis Wilson said publicly that he thought the matter was settled: "The vote can't change — it was too strong to one side."

Because I had such deep respect for the integrity, intelligence, and civic spirit of Lewis Wilson, I was much disturbed by his first-vote support of the right to arms provision. I could accept some votes on the committee without question, even when I disagreed. But I knew that Wilson voted out of conviction. I was hopeful that when the inevitable second vote on the section was taken by our committee, Wilson would change his mind and be with us. Surely he would realize before it was too late the chances we were taking by any unseemly encouragement of the use of guns. Interviewed by his home town newspaper, he confessed his misgivings, while asserting the relatively innocuous nature of the provision. He said: "In my opinion as a lawyer, it pretty well just puts into words what has already been written into law." It "leaves regulatory power to the state legislature," he suggested, adding a significant afterthought: "I said when I voted for the provision that if I learn it will not permit legislation to outlaw handguns, I will change my vote." If the legislature could not enact laws to prohibit concealed weapons or prevent ownership of guns by minors, felons, or mental incompetents, he would take a second look at the matter. He resented the *Chicago Sun-Times* editorial misstating, in his judgment, the effect of the proposed section. The usually placid Dallin Oaks also rebuked the press for misstating the situation as to similar provisions in other states. Until I had come to the convention, I had never realized the depth of feeling on this subject.

I tried to know what was going on in the various camps of the convention when important issues were at stake. At the time nothing appeared more important than the maneuvering over the right to arms provision. When the struggle was over and the issue appeared less important to me, I asked Clifford Downen, a young delegate from the southern part of the state, to tell me what actually happened. Downen was a leader in the fight for a permissive gun provision. When he testified before our committee, he threatened disaster if we did not yield. The threat delivered in Downen's habitual mild tone was quite impressive. "I am confident," he wrote to me, "that all the Convention delegates and other interested people share with me the desire to have published and committed to history the behind the scenes and day-to-day routine of the Convention." He went on:

> The recollections I have of the gun clause controversy date back to the first few weeks of the Convention.
>
> I recall that Friedrich, Hendren, Durr and myself submitted separate proposals relating to firearms.
>
> Hendren, Durr and myself began polling various delegates on the matter. The consensus was, as I recall, that a proposal to prohibit gun registration or gunowners' registration laws would fall short of passage. However, it appeared likely that a simple statement relating to the right to keep and bear arms would have broad enough appeal to pass.
>
> By the time your Committee began debating this matter we generally were willing to concede the registration fight. Actually we were very dubious about the prospects of getting any kind of gun clause out of the Bill of Rights Committee. As you well know, predicting the outcome of any issue before the Bill of Rights Committee was at best a grave risk.
>
> I might add to this point that in all probability, if the Committee had failed to report out a gun clause a very serious and divisive debate would have ensued. A debate that could have served only to drive a wedge between blocs of delegates who later on were to join together on several key issues.
>
> The outcome of the Committee debate surprised almost everyone. Efforts to get a "hard count" in the Committee failed due to the

uncommitted members. Kelleghan, Lennon, Hutmacher, Macdonald and Lawlor were safe, but the question marks were Wilson,
Dvorak, Arrigo, Fennoy, and Pechous.

Arrigo finally broke the ice with his proposal adding the words,
"subject to the police power of the state." The fact that he was
the one that proposed this helped tremendously.

After the committee had accepted the Arrigo proposal, our main
task was simply to maintain continual nose counts and to keep
our people from attempting to reopen the question of registration
during the floor debate.

This in a nutshell is the story, as I recall it. I might add that the
nose count I kept was within three votes of the final outcome. The
count remained very stable from the point the Committee reported
out the gun clause until third reading had concluded.

If one had to name the organizations most active and useful in
advocating changes in the bill of rights, the Welfare Council of
Metropolitan Chicago would be at or near the top of the list, and
its representative in Springfield during the convention, Linda Mayer,
would get a special award. Miss Mayer observed all of the committees and the convention generally, but she reserved her special attention for the Bill of Rights Committee. She attended virtually all of
its meetings and took copious notes, certainly far more extensive
than the secretary's. Whenever one had to recheck on a matter, Miss
Mayer was readily available. She had a talent for not imposing
herself. Whether it was by temperament or a matter of calculated
shrewdness, Miss Mayer never made her presence or her views so
apparent as to create annoyance or misgivings. As the convention
progressed, I found myself more and more in consultation with her.
There was one matter very dear to her — the rights of the mentally
and physically handicapped. After the bill of rights came to the
floor of the convention containing a nondiscrimination clause not
specifically directed to the handicapped, we talked over the situation, she and I and sometimes Peter Tomei, who, now that his
committee had reported to the convention, busied himself with
many other proposals and fields of inquiry. Who would be the best
one to sponsor a proposal for nondiscrimination for the handicapped? Obviously, Tomei and I would lend our names to it, but
it was better to enlist one of the more conservative delegates, some-

one like young Richard Daley. I talked with Daley and seemed to persuade him to be the principal sponsor; so did Linda Mayer and, I am sure, Tomei. Between us Daley was committed, much to the annoyance, as it turned out, of some who should have been in our corner, James Kemp and William Lennon, the trade union officials who were delegates to the convention. Daley was an indispensable ingredient in our ultimate success, a long and complicated story. Unfortunately, Miss Mayer was away from Springfield and out of the country when the matter came to a climax. There were other occasions when she made herself felt, quietly, sincerely, with a soft approach. She carried with her the prestige of the Welfare Council and her own dedication.

At the beginning of the convention, the Welfare Council distributed several skillfully drafted proposals for revision of the bill of rights. One proposal, consistent with the Model State Constitution, called for the revision of the 1870 due process clause (section 2), so that it would include equal protection of the laws of the state and any subdivision thereof. To it, they also proposed the addition of the words: "No person shall be subject to any discrimination in his rights for or in employment, housing, public accommodation or public education, or in any other of his inherent and inalienable rights because of race, color, religion, national ancestry, sex, or physical or mental disability, by any individual or by any firm, corporation, or institution, or by the state or any agency or subdivision of the state." Without inquiring whether or not I agreed with each word of the proposal and satisfied that in general I was committed to it, I translated the Welfare Council proposal into my own member proposal and filed it with the convention. During the same period of time and later, other proposals in the area of nondiscrimination were filed, and during the course of the committee deliberation, Lewis Wilson came forth with his proposal, ultimately the one adopted by the convention. Other organizations as well lent support to the movement for nondiscrimination. Apparently, its time had come.

In another proposal the Welfare Council supported the prohibition of all interceptions of private communications, whether privately or by government, and the banning of all evidence obtained in violation thereof in both civil and criminal proceedings. Interestingly, they tied this subject matter and the usual prohibition of unreasonable searches and seizures with a prohibition against unreasonable arrest or detention. This proposal too I introduced as my member proposal, and it too was the subject of other member proposals and proposals that arose in committee deliberations, as well as suggestions by other organizations.

In yet other proposals, the Welfare Council urged that all persons be bailable — financial surety to be used only to assure the appearance of the accused at trial — and bail not be excessive; that no conviction result in punishment by death; that the 1870 provision as to right to remedy and justice be made mandatory; that the doctrine of sovereign immunity be eliminated and that the state make pecuniary compensation to those suffering financial loss by reasons of the violent acts of criminals or unlawful actions by law enforcement officers; that there be no provision in the constitution which grants, denies, or limits the right to own, possess, bear, or transfer firearms; and that the entire matter of firearms be regulated by law. In each instance, I utilized these suggestions as my personal member proposals, and other members made proposals in almost all of these areas.

This was the manner in which interest groups affected the deliberations of the convention. Some delegate like myself would find one of their suggestions worthy of attention and would adopt it. As I had done for the Welfare Council, so I did for the Chicago Bar Association. Thus, in some areas my member proposals were repetitious in whole or in part of other proposals I or others had filed; sometimes they were even contradictory in minor or major respects. I wanted to make certain that all suggestions I found meritorious could be considered by my committee and the convention under its rules.

Carole Kamin Bellows, the chairman of the Chicago Bar Association committee charged with responsibility for considering revision of the Illinois Bill of Rights, was much less reticent than Linda Mayer in her willingness to testify before our committee. This highly charming and intelligent young woman was by birth and marital associations more deeply committed to the law than any person I have ever known. Both of her parents, her two brothers (including delegate Malcolm Kamin), her husband, her father-in-law, her uncles, her brothers' family associates, all were lawyers and in one instance the most esteemed Justice of the Illinois Supreme Court. She had worked on both the Chicago and Illinois State Bar Associations' committees on the bill of rights and had authored and edited a pamphlet highly regarded on the subject, which she distributed to the members of the convention committee. Under her dedicated leadership the Chicago Bar Association committee had come up with enlightened suggestions for improvement of the Illinois Bill of Rights, and the suggestions were only slightly watered down by the association's board of managers. By my invitation she then appeared before us, together with Manly Mumford, to champion the bar proposals and to answer questions with respect to them. The bar favored the inclusion of an equal protection of the laws clause, limitations on interceptions of communications, provisions for nondiscrimination, the strengthening of the right to remedy and justice section, a ban on the death penalty, the deletion of references to libel in the freedom of press section, and other provisions strengthening the protection of the individual and clarifying much of the antiquated language.

Most members of our committee showed great courtesy to the bar representatives and were grateful for the light that Carole Bellows and Manly Mumford were able to cast on the problems before us. A few members, notably Kelleghan, acted almost as cross-examiners in a criminal prosecution. These few were dubious about the good faith of the bar representatives. Why had not the total membership, instead of the board of managers alone, considered and voted on the suggested changes? These misgivings were all the more surprising in the case of Kelleghan who was about to become president of the bar association of his county. Mrs. Bellows and her associates took everything smilingly, determined to win support rather than antagonize even the most unreasonable person. In my mind, they clearly won on points. Whether or not they were achieving votes for their views I could not be sure at that point.

Odas Nicholson came before the committee with a proposed new preamble and explained it in a skillful and persuasive manner that was calm and unruffled until Leonard Foster commented upon it somewhat caustically. The two always seemed to annoy each other. By a narrow vote, the Nicholson preamble was defeated. I was determined to resurrect this eloquent preamble for a variety of reasons based on principle as well as strategy. I counseled Miss Nicholson about a certain required blending between the 1870 preamble and her suggested redraft. I alerted Kemp about the necessity of his being present for the second vote on the Nicholson preamble some days later. To say that the atmosphere was charged is to understate the tensions of the second discussion and vote; the climax was utterly unexpected.

The proposed preamble now read:

> We the people of the state of Illinois, grateful to almighty God for our freedom, in order to provide for the health, safety and welfare of the people, maintain a representative and orderly government, eliminate inequality and poverty, assure legal, social and economic justice, provide opportunity for the fullest development of the individual and to secure the blessings of freedom and liberty, do ordain and establish this Constitution.

A motion was made to delete the reference to "elimination of poverty and inequality" as one of the goals set forth in the Nicholson preamble. It was defeated. Kelleghan moved to substitute the Alaska preamble for the Nicholson one, calling it "more brief and less controversial." Other committee members referred to the two state constitutions without preambles. Foster, not one to smooth over the situation, called the Nicholson proposal "brilliant in conception but miserable in execution."

The Nicholson preamble was approved 8 to 6, with Arrigo, Fennoy, Gertz, Kemp, Macdonald, Raby, Weisberg, and Wilson voting yes, Pechous absent, and the rest of the committee (Dvorak, Foster, Hutmacher, Kelleghan, Lawlor, and Lennon) voting no.

"Such a revision to gain the ends of government happens to be the fundamental principle of socialism," Kelleghan later said. "Goals of economic justice and equality pursued by themselves and without reliance upon God are the goals of socialism."

"No other state in the union has adopted such a radical expression of governmental purpose, nor do they embrace the goals of socialism. It is to be hoped that this new preamble will be defeated on the floor of the convention and that Illinois will retain its cherished constitutional ideas, so well expressed in the state's present preamble."

Suddenly after the vote, Foster got up and declared he was no longer the secretary of the committee; he was resigning. Later he commented to the press as to me: "He is the most incompetent supervisor I've ever had and I won't work with him. He interferes." I refused to be drawn into any controversy on the subject, saying only that I had not asked for Foster's resignation and would not ask him to reconsider. I characterized him as "temperamental" and said the work of the committee must go on, regardless of personalities. I appointed Virginia Macdonald, so wise and calm in her bearing — and with the ability to operate a tape recorder! — as Foster's successor, at least for the time being. Her local newspaper quoted Mrs. Macdonald as believing both Foster and myself temperamental. "I'm counting on us working out the differences before Tuesday and getting things back in order when we reconvene," she said. "Len Foster has contributed a great deal to our committee and it will be a real shame if we cannot get him to reconsider. This was a personality conflict that I think can be worked out."

The episode created considerably more excitement than essentially more important matters. It led to my one heated exchange with the executive director of the convention and upset me more than I cared to admit. Bernard Weisberg urged me to "cool it," and I tried to do so.

While we were still struggling in our committee to achieve harmony, so that we might produce at last our report on the bill of rights, I was asked to deliver the invocation one day at the opening of a plenary session of the convention. There is poignancy in the words I uttered on March 26, 1970 — the first prayer I had ever composed. I thought of our committee and particularly some wilful members as I intoned:

> Gracious God, who moves mighty mountains and has eternity in which to work, teach us who are less than mountains and are limited in time and talents — teach us Thy wisdom, Thy patience, Thy forebearance and charity — teach us so that we may complete the great task assigned to us by Thy people. Teach us that it is not the shrill voice, but softness and silence even, that persuades. Teach us that we are fallible, that we must reconcile our differences of

viewpoint and personality. Through Thy grace, may we achieve the collective will and wisdom that are necessary if we are to produce a great charter for our state, preserving all that is worthy in the past and daring to proclaim all that is necessary to make the future a true treasure for our posterity. May we take great joy in the adventure of working together and with Thee. *Amen.*

It would require daring to create a preamble that would express such high hopes; for as I said when our committee was in session and later to the convention, in the words of the poet Browning: "Our reach should exceed our grasp, or what's a Heaven for!"

It was only natural that many people were fearful that the Bill of Rights Committee would not resolve its many differences. The *Chicago Tribune* wrote about the situation at times almost as if they relished the dilemma of Gertz and his committee. Generally, it contented itself with minor digs; on May 3, 1970, it published an extensive account of the difficulties as it and undoubtedly many others saw them. The gloomy tone was set immediately:

> Of the constitutional convention's nine major committees, undoubtedly the most controversial and least predictable is the bill of rights committee.
> So far, its decisions have ranged across the political spectrum — from liberal proposals guaranteeing open housing and banning all wire tapping to conservative measures assuring the individual's right to own and use firearms, and asserting an unborn child's right to life.
> In the last four months, committee members have engaged in angry shouting matches, threatened resignation and revolt, and conducted behind-the-scene intrigue which would put most cloak-and-dagger novelists to shame.

John Elmer dwelt at length on the "executive session" over the "perpetual dilemma" as to Larry Miller. It will be remembered that this private session had come on the insistence of Kemp, the vice-chairman, but the *Tribune* attributed it to me, adding: "Some observers feared for the fate of the public's right to know." Because of my life-long devotion to freedom of expression, this was a cruel blow. There was worse: "While maintaining an outward appearance of openness, the committee has indulged in some clandestine activities common to more authoritarian groups — especially by stamping a top-secret label on some committee documents."

There followed a slanted account of the documents, thus far withheld principally because Dallin Oaks wanted to be able to communicate candidly with the committee. The account concluded: "Since the secrecy of the papers has been reduced mostly to silliness, they probably will be made public next week." Worse followed:

> Gertz, a liberal Democrat, has had trouble leading the committee, largely because of personality conflicts. More than once his rulings have been rejected by the committee.
>
> His chief antagonist has been Thomas C. Kelleghan of West Chicago, a conservative Republican with a volatile temper.
>
> But a fellow Democrat, Leonard N. Foster of Chicago, also has made Gertz' job an unenviable one. An assistant corporation counsel with an independent streak, Foster once quit as committee secretary, announcing he could no longer work under Gertz but later reconsidered.
>
> The Rev. Francis X. Lawlor of Chicago, conservative Catholic priest, has unnerved Gertz and other committee members from time to time, once by bringing a jar containing the remains of a fetus to the committee room to illustrate his views on abortion.

Then, almost as if fearing there was over-simplification by blaming Gertz alone, the article went on: "A look at the composition of the committee gives some insight into its unpredictability." The membership was then named and briefly categorized, person by person. The conclusion was ominous:

> While the committee has had its troubles, the individuality of its members has made for some startling philosophical switches on the issues.
>
> When the over-all report reaches the floor, it is likely that the battle of the bill of rights committee will be waged all over again.[1]

Such things at times affected the morale of the convention staff. The assistant clerk later told me that she had expressed her fears to the clerk, Gerald Sbarboro. He said to her: "Don't be afraid. Gertz in the end will bring in an acceptable report." I was glad to

[1] John Elmer, "Bill of Rights for Con-Con Argumentative," *Chicago Tribune,* May 3, 1970.

learn that not everyone had been so trepidatious! When, in the end, our committee became, in retrospect, almost a model for the convention as to how to conduct ourselves during convention debate, and many members voiced their enthusiastic praise, I sometimes felt like asking, "Where were you when we needed you?"

Regardless as to whether I agreed or disagreed with the results on any issues in our committee, I was almost invariably philosophical, and grateful when "our side" was victorious, especially when the vote was unexpected. I must confess that on a few occasions I was shocked and grieved. Once I spoke angrily to the member of the committee with whom I felt personally closest, because that member voted, incomprehensibly, for a viewpoint that I thought was utterly mischievous. There was one vote that disturbed me even more than the gun vote, the one that led to the inclusion, at the committee report stage, of the phrase, "including the unborn," in the due process clause. I was taken completely by surprise. There seemed a kind of effrontery in the vote, an imposition upon people of good will; not even our ultimate triumph in the convention could wipe out the memory. Another embarrassment came when the committee insisted upon maintaining the unconstitutional clause on truth in libel in the freedom of speech section. That lawyers led the successful fight for inclusion of the language, both in the committee and the convention, has never ceased to puzzle me. Great as was my joy in our final product, it was not unalloyed, because of this unwise language, a thumbing of our noses at the United States Supreme Court. Nobody could have expected so few sad moments for one who aspired to the production of a great charter of individual rights.

A few weeks before we submitted our report to the convention, I was asked by a legal publication to write about the Bill of Rights Committee and its work for a Law Day issue. When I wrote I could not be sure of the final product of our efforts, either in committee or in convention, or how the voters would respond. The words I then wrote have an intimacy and perhaps a natural eloquence that nothing written months later can achieve. It is worth repeating them here for the light then shed on my hopes and fears at the time when everything hung in the balance. For ease of reading, I have refrained from inserting quotation marks in the passages from my own article. I have interpolated nothing, except as indicated by brackets. The passages are as I then wrote them:

There were many, including organized labor, who opposed the calling of a constitutional convention in Illinois, because they feared that it would produce a regressive document, particularly with respect to the bill of rights. They demanded that the bill of rights be unchanged or, if changed, that it be simply a replica of the federal Bill of Rights. I understood, I still understand, their fears.

When I ran for election as a member of the convention, I said that I would not necessarily be bound to support its end-product; that if the proposed new charter were worse than the old one, I would oppose it. There was a very real possibility of a disaster.

When I was unexpectedly elected, I never thought I would head any of the committees of the convention because of the political realities. When I permitted myself to reflect wishfully about the matter, I felt that I would rather be chairman of the Bill of Rights Committee than president of the convention.

And, somehow, I became chairman of that committee, with fifteen members the second largest committee of the convention and, in some respects, the most diversified in viewpoint and personality.

It contains white and black persons, lawyers and laymen, Jews and Gentiles, Catholics and various shades of Protestants, not to mention the irreligious, Goldwater Republicans and New Deal Democrats, and everything in between, the flexible and the inflexible, the gracious and the grim.

How was I to steer such a group in one general direction in order to produce an acceptable charter of basic individual rights?

If one reads the press, one is skeptical about the prospect of getting anywhere. For example, on the very day that the media depicted Father Lawlor and the chairman as being hopelessly at odds, he and I were dining together in the friendliest manner with one of our conservative colleagues.

We will not agree on everything. We will agree on enough to produce something worth supporting.

One member of the committee, a veteran of the General Assembly and a man of great culture, has said that being a member of the committee has been the most fascinating experience of his life, a view echoed by others.

The committee has been fortunate in its choice of special counsel — Professor Dallin Oaks of the University of Chicago Law School. Despite his youth, Professor Oaks has had a very distinguished career, which has included serving as law clerk of Chief Justice Warren, consultant to the Department of Justice under Attorney General Mitchell, and, starting next September, director of the American Bar Association Foundation.

Conservative in viewpoint, he has the ability to reconcile opposites. He has been of invaluable assistance to the chairman in bridging the gaps and reconciling differences.

The committee has the so-called seven day rule. This means that no decision is final until a week has elapsed. Within that period, any member may ask for a new vote.

[I then summarized, section by section, what we had agreed upon as of the time of my writing. Nothing is gained by repeating those passages of the article. I went on:]

Thus, even if we do nothing more, we are leaving the bill of rights better than we found it, certainly not worsened (except with respect to the right to bear arms). We may go beyond the present charter in several additional respects.

I am confident that we will add an environmental bill of rights that is more than hortatory in nature, and we may declare the right of every person to the necessities of life (food, clothing, shelter, education, medical care), but this latter will be a pious principle rather than a reality.

After our committee has rendered its report, majority and minority, it will be up to the committee of the whole of the convention to debate the merits and demerits of what we propose. One cannot be absolutely certain how any undisciplined delegate body will react.

I am confident, however, that what is best in our proposals will survive, what is unwise will perish. At any rate, there will have been a recurrence to fundamental principles and the rest will be up to the sovereign people.

Dozens of proposals were submitted to our committee on every aspect of contemporary life. Hundreds of persons testified before us in Chicago, Waukegan, various other parts of the state, and especially in Springfield, the seat of the convention. We received countless communications.

Some people were deferential to us, others accusatory and demanding. There were some subjects that aroused tremendous feeling — the rights of women, aid to non-public schools, the bearing of arms, environmental pollution, abortion.

Many felt that we ought to insert all sorts of new provisions, even if we only sermonized, rather than granting rights. Some refused to recognize that a constitution is not a set of statutes.

Others wanted to leave everything to the General Assembly, nothing to the Convention. One cannot understand the democratic process unless one has gone through our experience.

One day the new constitution will be either accepted or rejected, in whole or in part. The document itself will never be complete. The whole story can be known only by those who participated in its making. They should tell that story as a contribution to popular education.

[And this I am trying to do in the present treatise, which resumes in regular order.]

IV

The Committee Reports to the Convention

President Witwer had been urging the Bill of Rights Committee to file its full report or at least a substantial segment of it without delay. "Urging" is perhaps too mild a word. He came as near to insistence as one could without actually issuing an order. Many on the committee were annoyed, even outraged, by the pressure being put on us. We felt that we were diligent and conscientious and acting with reasonable dispatch and that we had gone far beyond the call of duty. We were notorious for the long hours we devoted to our work, and the uninhibited nature of our discussion. The chairman was often described as a Simon Legree in his cracking of the whip.

At last we neared the point of consummation, and the chairman became as eager as the president of the convention to file a report. Portions of the report were prepared as we labored on other matters. Drafts of sections and then of the whole report were given to all members of the committee, and they were urged to give their definitive comments on each section and page. We had a subcommittee headed by Lewis Wilson work with Dallin Oaks on the draft. Formal notices of a deadline were sent out. A final meeting was held. Still a few, notably Foster, felt that more time was required. After the final meeting, I became adamant and declared that the report would be filed, despite anyone. The convention staff was cooperative and we proceeded with great speed, despite Foster. He refused to sign the report and made an issue of the matter on the floor of the convention. The president supported me. Kelleghan too failed to sign although he was aware of the deadline. He also raised the issue on the floor of the convention. I refused to quarrel with him. I pointed out that more than the requisite majority had signed the report and authorized its filing. Again the president sustained me. In neither instance did any member of the committee or the convention take up the cudgels for Foster or Kelleghan. As a matter of fact, with their permission, I had signed for two of the committee members besides myself — Vice-chairman Kemp, who was away on trade union business, and Weisberg, who had an illness in his family. In time, the minor controversy was forgotten. There were more important things to argue over!

One of these things was the order of presentation in the committee of the whole of the separate sections. The logical way, perhaps, was to start with the preamble and then go on to the various sections of the bill of rights in numerical order. Virtually all of the committee members felt that this would be highly prejudicial. Arrigo, for one, felt that his favorite proposal on individual dignity might go down the drain unless it were protected. We had a subcommittee, on which the vice-chairman sat, consider the matter, and they reported to the full committee. Then another subcommittee, on which the chairman sat, went over the matter again. Finally, an order was agreed upon. We would first present those sections as to which we were unanimous and then the more contested ones, starting with those sections that were unchanged. I saw no harm and much good in a special order of presentation. President Witwer initially disagreed with us in an insistent manner, but when he realized how strongly we felt and that trouble might ensue, he yielded, and we were given leave to present the sections in the order we deemed most appropriate. In my judgment we turned out to be right. Although first reading debate on the bill of rights consumed portions of eight days, it took much less time than if we had plunged into acrimonious discussion of highly controversial sections — for example, the rights of the unborn. We got the less divisive sections out of the way with little trouble.

Our counsel Dallin Oaks drafted the majority report, but he had the benefit of the thinking of each of us on the committee. No one could reasonably claim that he had been slighted. Our report pointed out that the committee had given almost twenty weeks of intensive consideration to the task assigned to it. The committee had received eighty-one member proposals from President Witwer, many combining a wide variety of subjects and some confined to one or a few ideas. We listed all of these proposals. We told of the more than two hundred fifty witnesses we had heard, most of whom were not members of the convention; and we listed their names, affiliations, and subject matters. The witnesses ranged from true experts to zealots; some supporting, some opposing, the various proposals. We listed the vast amount of written material we had received and considered, some of the best being the fifty L.A.R.A.M.s. We told of our debt, as did other committee reports, to the Braden and Cohn analysis of the Illinois Constitution of 1870. We pointed out that our committee dealt, as was obvious, with a large number of controversial issues. Notwithstanding the dangerous areas in which we trod, we decided some issues — nine sections indeed — by unanimous vote. We recommended the retention unchanged of twelve of the original twenty sections of the article. True, we urged amendment of the preamble and eight sections, and we added seven new sections. In some instances, the vote was very close and sometimes changed between the first vote and the second, permitted under the special rules of our committee. We could truthfully say, as suggested by Arthur Lennon: "In all cases the issues were squarely faced, vigorously debated, and firmly decided."

It was now up to the convention to dispose of what we had proposed.

The report contained a table, prepared by Leonard Foster, which showed the votes of the members of the committee in comparative form. It indicated that there were twenty-eight basic propositions on which final votes were taken, this after the many "first votes" and the many trial runs on amendments. Victor Arrigo and William Fennoy had identical records, although not necessarily voting always the same way. Each had missed only one vote and had never passed any. They had voted yes twenty-four times and no only three times on the various sections that had been adopted. John Dvorak and Virginia Macdonald were next in the order of conformity with the winning vote, each having twenty-three yes votes and Mrs. Macdonald only two no votes and Dvorak three; their absences were two and one, respectively. Both Kelleghan, who in the end voted against the constitution, and Father Lawlor, who favored it, had twenty-two yes votes, but Kelleghan had six no votes and the good father only four. So far as yes voting was concerned, the others were grouped around twenty-one and twenty, the exceptions being Weisberg with fifteen and Kemp with sixteen. There was a basic difference between Weisberg and Kemp. The latter, in the end, opposed the constitution but he voted no only once on the basic issues, while Weisberg voted no nine times. Foster was the great dissenter, ten times casting no votes. Wilson had nine no votes, Hutmacher eight, and Lennon and Raby seven. Thus analyzed, there was a great degree of consensus, only a few members departing from this norm. None had more dissents than approvals from the majority vote.

There was discussion — sometimes acrimonious — at several committee meetings as to the manner, in addition to the order, of presentation of the various sections of the preamble and bill of rights. It was assumed that the chairman would lead off the discussion and give an over-all account of the article and our work in connection with it, and that he would be up front in the convention hall, prepared to field the discussion and answer questions not handled by other members of the committee. Some, I am sure, particularly the more conservative, were concerned as to what I might say; others, including some who did not always vote with me, were less or not at all concerned. There was a point at which I brushed aside more specific inquiry or efforts at censorship and assured the committee that I was well aware as to what was required of me. I had in mind the brilliant lead-off by Peter Tomei, when he presented the report of his committee, the very first to come before the committee of the whole. Tomei was fully master of everything involved in the report — its origins, its rationale, why it should be adopted by the convention. His voice was strong, his diction and enunciation good, his tone assured; it was a masterly performance — a guide to other committee chairmen.

It was my feeling, acquiesced in by almost all of the committee members, that each one on the committee ought to make one or more presentations. There were enough sections for all. The question was how and to whom to distribute them. Some were natural choices. Who, if not Victor Arrigo, ought to discuss the section on individual dignity? He was willing, indeed. Somewhat to the same extent, William Fennoy was responsible for the inclusion of a section on preliminary hearings in criminal matters. True, he was not a lawyer. At first, he agreed to present the section; then he had afterthoughts and suggested, wisely, that Bernard Weisberg ought to present the matter. It was easy to think of Arthur Lennon as leading in the discussion on due process, "including the unborn." He had evolved those highly charged words. And so it went with each section. When there was not an obvious choice, we turned the matter over to one who had no other assignment, or few. Sometimes when a section was turned over to a member, he would seek counsel from another member. Virginia Macdonald, given the horatory first section with its Declaration of Independence derivations, called in Victor Arrigo to work with her, meaning that an unopposed section had great oratory, scholarship, and prolixity to support it.

To my surprise, the vice-chairman James Kemp chose not to present any section to the convention although he said that in several instances, as with the nondiscrimination section, he would back up the presentation from the floor. Who then was our best resource on the matter of nondiscrimination? Of course Lewis Wilson, originally dubious about the matter and then the one most determined to see it through. In a sense, I smacked my lips in anticipation of the effectiveness of Wilson's presentation.

Thomas Kelleghan would not present any section. I cannot say that I was wholly sad over this in view of his votes and vocal chastisement of those who disagreed with him. His intention seemed formed to oppose the constitution.

Some members were so well qualified that the problem was one of limitation. Weisberg, the great advocate of individual rights, could have been the spokesman for many sections. Knowing that he would present some of the minority reports, we had to curtail what was assigned to him.

Leonard Foster was extremely eager, sometimes too eager, to make presentations. Brilliant and informed, however erratic, he could be given several assignments, and was.

What was there to do about Father Lawlor when one was uncomfortable as to what he might say? He was assigned the section on freedom of assembly.

The committee was stiff-necked about utilizing nonmembers of the Bill of Rights Committee for presentations. I suggested that Odas Nicholson, who after all was largely responsible for the revised preamble, be our representative up front for this purpose. No, it had to be a committee member. The same was true with respect to the public employees section; I could not officially designate Mary Lee Leahy. I did call upon Miss Nicholson and Mrs. Leahy from their seats.

So in the end everyone who wanted an assignment was satisfied, and we were prepared to give good accounts of ourselves.

PREAMBLE

The committee report took up the proposed preamble and bill of rights item by item, attempting to give the justification for each item and summarizing the viewpoint of the opposition and, briefly, other member proposals that it considered.

Starting with the preamble, the report set forth that the committee voted 8 to 6 (with 1 absent) to substitute the following preamble for the 1870 preamble:

> *We, the people of the State of Illinois — grateful to Almighty God for the civil, political and religious liberty which He hath so long permitted us to enjoy, and looking to Him for a blessing upon our endeavors — in order to provide for the health, safety and welfare of the people, maintain a representative and orderly government, eliminate poverty and inequality, establish and assure legal, social and economic justice, provide opportunity for the fullest development of the individual, insure domestic tranquility, provide for the common defense, and secure the blessings of freedom and liberty to ourselves and our posterity; do ordain and establish this Constitution for the State of Illinois.*

"This Preamble," the report said, "attempts to preserve the essential characteristics of the 1870 Preamble, but supplements it with phrases that express the concerns and aspirations of the people of the State of Illinois in this second half of the Twentieth Century."

The report gave, in specific terms, the similarities and differences between the 1870 preamble and the proposed new one. It pointed out that the new preamble was an adaption of one member proposal and was consistent with another one.

Yet another proposal had "suggested a new Preamble that would have acknowledged a common brotherhood under God and would have recognized a special obligation to protect the young, the aged, the weak, and the poor and to guarantee that all would have access to adequate food, medicine, clothing, shelter and undefiled environment." This was much like proposals that had been made and rejected for specific sections in the bill of rights itself.

Four other proposals had suggested retention of the 1870 preamble, and a minority of the committee supported that viewpoint. They thought it inappropriate to change the phraseology of something so basic as the century-old statement of the purposes of the constitution. They objected, moreover, on stylistic grounds to the blending of modern phraseology with the traditional wording of the existing preamble. They were doubtful that some of the new matters were proper governmental objectives. As the report phrased it: "Even though a Preamble is hortatory in nature and does not create any substantive rights, the minority opposed the expression of these questionable objectives because they were concerned that their presence in the Preamble might influence the interpretation of substantive rights granted elsewhere in the Constitution and statutes of the State."

It will be remembered that Kelleghan had suggested in the committee deliberations that the proposed new language was revolutionary. The report did not go that far in summarizing the minority viewpoint.

INHERENT AND INALIENABLE RIGHTS

The report pointed out that the committee voted 14 to 0 (with 1 absent) to retain unchanged section 1 of the 1870 bill of rights:

> *All men are by nature free and independent, and have certain inherent and inalienable rights — among these are life, liberty and the pursuit of happiness. To secure these rights and the protection of property, governments are instituted among men, deriving their just powers from the consent of the governed.*

As the report indicated, this was familiar phraseology from the Declaration of Independence, widely accepted and appropriate for inclusion at the outset of the bill of rights. It was indicated that most state constitutions had similar verbiage.

One proposal, originally approved by the committee, had added the word "privacy" after the word "liberty." This was a valid expression of the concern in that area, but when the section on search and seizure was expanded in the same spirit, the insertion was deleted so that the familiar phrase, "life, liberty and the pursuit of happiness," remained untouched.

One of my proposals would have added a requirement that the constitution, and particularly the preamble and the bill of rights, be interpreted and implemented to secure these inherent and inalienable rights. Another proposal would have deleted a portion of the section.

DUE PROCESS AND EQUAL PROTECTION

The report went on to say that the committee had voted 9 to 6 to substitute the following provision in place of section 2 of the 1870 bill of rights:

> *No person, including the unborn, shall be deprived of life, liberty or property, without due process of law; nor shall any person be denied the equal protection of the law.*

It was noted that the first clause of the provision followed the familiar phraseology of the 1870 bill of rights, the due process clause, except (and the exception made all of the difference in the world) that the new provision added the words, "including the unborn."

The second clause adopted an equal protection clause, something completely new in the Illinois Constitution and contained in only a few state constitutions. The addition of an equal protection clause had been frequently suggested, there being no less than eight member proposals along that line.

As was pointed out in the report, section 1 of the Fourteenth Amendment to the United States Constitution forbade any state from denying the equal protection of the laws to any person within its jurisdiction. In giving effect to the provision and similar principles in the 1870 constitution prohibiting laws granting special privileges or immunities or denying due process of law (such as Art. II, sec. 2; Art. II, sec. 14; Art. IV, sec. 22), the Illinois courts have frequently applied the rule against denying equal protection of the law. Therefore, it was opined, the addition of an equal protection clause simply gave formal expression to a well recognized and applied principle. The committee unanimously considered such inclusion desirable for the sake of clarity and completeness.

The committee was also unanimous in retaining the provision as to due process of law, believing that it embodied guarantees so all-encompassing and potent as not to require further explanation.

Then the report went on to discuss the new words, "including the unborn." These, it said, were meant to assure that an unborn person cannot be deprived of life, liberty, or property by the state without due process of law. It contended that the provision was not intended to regulate private individual relationships. It admitted that the rights of the unborn — as against the interests of the parents, other relatives, and society as a whole — were a matter of sharp controversy at this time. It said that Illinois judicial decisions were incomplete in this area. It maintained that the new words made certain that there would be continuing efforts to resolve the problems. A member proposal, adapted in committee by Arthur Lennon, had declared that the inalienable right to life should be protected through due process of law in all cases involving the innocent, the aged, the ill, the insane, and the unborn fetus. This was Father Lawlor's all-encompassing program. It was made more palatable by Lennon.

Six members of the committee had voted against inclusion of this new language. As the report indicated briefly, they urged the indefiniteness of the critical word "unborn," the negative effects which they asserted such a constitutional provision would have on current efforts to reform abortion laws and deal with population control, and the inadvisability of making any changes in a provision so important and familiar as the due process clause. As we shall see when the minority report is considered, this was only the bare bones of the minority viewpoint. It was clear that a real battle would ensue on the floor of the convention.

Religious Freedom

Then the report returned to what was on the surface less controversial ground. The committee had voted 13 to 0 (with 2 absent) to retain unchanged section 3 of the 1870 bill of rights:

> *The free exercise and enjoyment of religious profession and worship, without discrimination, shall forever be guaranteed; and no person shall be denied any civil or political right, privilege or capacity, on account of his religious opinions; but the liberty of conscience hereby secured shall not be construed to dispense with oaths or affirmations, excuse acts of licentiousness, or justify practices inconsistent with the peace or safety of the State. No person shall be required to attend or support any ministry or place of worship against his consent, nor shall any preference be given by law to any religious denomination or mode of worship.*

As the report said, the committee was persuaded of the inadvisability of changing even one word in this sensitive and vital provision. It had heard many witnesses on this subject and the related one in the education article (Article VIII, sec. 3). It was underscored that whether witnesses were for or against government aid to private schools, they feared changes that would work against their respective positions. Considering the deep concern on the subject, the report was sparse and circumspect in what it had to say, merely pointing out the high priority of the problem and the contemplated legislative proposals and litigation. Almost gingerly the report opined "that the existing provision adequately and clearly guarantees religious freedom and provides for the separation of Church and State."

It made passing reference to two proposals that suggested retention of portions of the existing section and two that would have substituted the language of the First Amendment of the United States Constitution.

Freedom of Speech

By reason of rulings in the reviewing courts of the state and nation, what was said about freedom of speech had considerable significance. Despite one court ruling, the committee had voted 11 to 4 to retain unchanged section 4 of the 1870 bill of rights:

> *Every person may freely speak, write and publish on all subjects,*
> *being responsible for the abuse of that liberty; and in all trials for*
> *libel, both civil and criminal, the truth, when published with good*
> *motives and for justifiable ends, shall be a sufficient defense.*

It was pointed out that approximately three-quarters of the state constitutions had free speech and press guarantees in terms similar to the quoted first clause, and a majority of such state provisions treated the subject of truth as a defense to libel.

Almost peremptorily, the report said: "The prime consideration in rejecting various proposals to change the second clause was the Committee's desire to make no change in the existing rules governing the circumstances in which truth is a defense to libel."

One proposal would have substituted for this section the language of the First Amendment to the United States Constitution. Two proposals would have deleted the whole second clause, thus omitting all reference to libel. One proposal would have said nothing about good motives and justifiable ends, so that truth would be a sufficient defense in all libel cases. These alternatives were rejected, the report said, because in the absence of a constitutional provision referring to libel or limiting the circumstances in which truth was a defense, truth would be a complete defense in an action for civil libel, but not in a prosecution for criminal defamation when good motives and justifiable ends were required by the statutes.[1]

The effect of the United States Supreme Court decisions in *New York Times* v. *Sullivan*[2] and succeeding cases was discussed. It was recognized that in order to protect free speech and press, a plaintiff could not recover damages for a defamatory statement involving the conduct of a public official or a discussion of public affairs unless the plaintiff proved that the statements were false and made with "actual malice." It was recognized at least formally that in *Farnsworth* v. *Tribune Co.,*[3] a case lost by the committee chairman himself, the Illinois Supreme Court had held that the portion of section 4 dealing with libel was unconstitutional under the First Amendment to the United States Constitution insofar as it qualified the defense of truth in a civil libel action by a "public figure" or in-

[1] *Illinois Revised Statutes*, 1969, ch. 38, sec. 827–2.
[2] 376 U.S. 254 (1964).
[3] 43 Ill. 2d 286, 253 N.E. 2d 408 (1969).

volving "matters of public interest." Nonetheless, the committee stuck to the 1870 language although the chairman had almost cheerfully recognized that the viewpoint he had unsuccessfully advocated as plaintiff's attorney in the *Farnsworth* case was no longer valid in Illinois or elsewhere.

The report pointed out that a minority of the committee would have replaced the second clause of section 4 with language intended to preserve the terms of the truth defense to the maximum extent possible, but conforming with the rulings of the United States Supreme Court. As the report suggested, the majority was concerned that the minority provision would have the effect of making changes not actually required by the new rulings.

TRIAL BY JURY

The report went on to discuss another subject of great interest, trial by jury, and the committee voted 10 to 4 (with 1 passing) to delete the concluding clause but otherwise to retain unchanged section 5 of the 1870 bill of rights:

The right of trial by jury as heretofore enjoyed shall remain inviolate.

The new provision was identical (except for a correction in punctuation) to the first clause in section 5 of the 1870 bill of rights. The second clause of the old section, providing that a jury of less than twelve men might be authorized by law for "the trial of civil cases before a justice of the peace," was deleted as of doubtful validity since justice of the peace courts were abolished by constitutional amendment.

While forty-six states guaranteed that the right to trial by jury would remain inviolate, the provisions varied widely in language and substance, with many exceptions as to civil actions and the amount in dispute. There were differences in about half of the states as to the number of jurors who must concur in order to render a verdict in civil cases, ten constitutions specifying the necessary number and fourteen others giving the legislature authority.

As the report recorded, the committee considered and rejected all sorts of proposals. It went so far as to modify the right to trial by jury "in suits between private persons for damages for death or injury to persons or property," giving the General Assembly authority to prescribe new methods of determining facts in civil cases in order to combat congestion and other problems in the courts. Then the committee changed its collective mind, believing that the problems could be solved by administrative and legislative reforms without weakening fundamental jury trial guarantees. Four members did favor permitting the General Assembly to "provide for juries of less than twelve persons in lesser civil cases and petty offenses."

There were many suggestions by the members of the convention. Four dealt with criminal cases. One proposal would have given the legislature power to provide for trials by juries of less than twelve and without a unanimous verdict where the offense was not punishable by death or by imprisonment in the penitentiary. Another proposal would have permitted juries of from six to twelve in all criminal cases. Two others required the concurrence of nine of twelve or twelve of fifteen jurors for conviction in the trial of all criminal proceedings.

Six suggestions concerned the right of trial by jury in civil cases. Two proposals would have given the legislature power to authorize juries of from six to twelve in all civil cases. Two other proposals stated that juries of less than twelve could be authorized by law in civil cases. Another proposal made the same provision as to civil cases and traffic offenses. A proposal empowered the legislature to provide for less than unanimous verdicts. Two other proposals accepted this concept, but also specified that at least three-fourths of the jury must concur in a verdict.

Chief Justice Underwood of the Illinois Supreme Court had written to the chairman after the committee deliberations were completed. He and certain other justices wanted a good deal of easing of the jury requirements, but the committee was indisposed to go too far. The matter would obviously come up again during debate on the floor of the convention.

SEARCHES, SEIZURES, INTERCEPTIONS, AND PRIVACY

The report then discussed some of the far-reaching changes incorporated in section 6. The committee voted 10 to 3 (with 1 passing and 1 absent) to substitute a new first clause, and the committee voted 9 to 3 (with 3 absent) to retain the second clause unchanged:

> *The right of the people to be secure in their persons, houses, papers and other possessions against unreasonable searches, seizures, interceptions of their communications, by eavesdropping devices or other means, or invasions of their privacy shall not be violated; and no warrant shall issue without probable cause, supported by affidavit, particularly describing the place to be searched, and the persons or things to be seized.*

The report recounted that forty-five state constitutions had provisions substantially similar to section 6 of the 1870 bill of rights, all of these following the language in the Fourth Amendment to the United States Constitution. The new section went beyond the old provision in two important respects. It added a right against "interceptions of their communications by eavesdropping devices or other means," and a right against "invasions of their privacy." This was a matter of the greatest public concern treated, if at all, in few state constitutions. New York was the only one with a constitutional provision — promising more than it delivered — on eavesdropping. It prohibited "unreasonable interception of telephone and telegraph communications," unless upon judicial order issued on probable cause. Arizona and Washington were the two states which mentioned privacy in their constitutions, declaring that "no person shall be disturbed in his private affairs, or his home invaded, without authority of law."

The report identified the changes in the section:

(1) The words "other possessions," used instead of the word "effects" in the first clause, embodied court decisions on the scope of the freedom from unreasonable search and seizure.

(2) The words "interceptions of their communications by eavesdropping devices or other means" in the first clause created a right in respect to interception of communications similar to the prohibition against "unreasonable searches and seizures." Initially the committee voted to forbid "any interception of their communications by eavesdropping devices," even with the consent of one party, as provided in the *Illinois Revised Statutes*.[4] Then the committee voted

[4] 1969, ch. 38, sec. 14-2.

the more flexible provision. Its interpretation requires a case-by-case adjudication as with unreasonable searches and seizures. The addition of the words "or other means" made certain that the prohibition applied to all interceptions of communications, whether or not by "eavesdropping devices." This minimum guarantee may be made more stringent by the General Assembly. As the report underscored, some on the committee opposed this provision because they still favored an absolute ban on all interceptions and thought that the word "unreasonable" might permit wiretapping or other eavesdropping practices beyond what was presently permitted. Others thought the present legislation adequate.

(3) The words "invasions of their privacy" are self-evident as used in the first clause. Nobody can wholly escape personal intrusions in this crowded and complicated world with its manifold responsibilities and technological developments. Despite all, it was strongly felt that it was essential to the dignity and well being of the individual that there be a zone of privacy not subject to disclosure or review by government or public officials.

Some on the committee felt that the second clause (providing for the issuance of warrants) should encompass the new guarantees as well as the old, but the majority was unpersuaded, and the clause was not changed.

As with the other sections, the report briefly considered the proposals that had been submitted to the committee. Two proposals preferred keeping the 1870 provision. One proposal preferred phrasing the guarantee as a right to be "secure in their right of privacy against unreasonable searches, seizures, disclosures, interception of communications and other invasions of privacy." Another proposal included a guarantee against "any interception of their oral or other communications." One was phrased as a right to be secure against "unreasonable interception of telephone, telegraph and other electronic communications and against unreasonable interception of oral and other communications by electric or electronic methods," but permitted a presiding judge to issue an order for interception upon affidavit and with the consent of the attorney general or state's attorney.

Going beyond that, one proposal, submitted by the chairman, provided that where freedom of expression was involved there could be no search or seizure until after an adversary judicial proceeding to determine the propriety of the search or seizure. Along a different line, another proposal guaranteed access to personal credit and financial data in the hands of financial, credit, and accounting institutions. Another proposal guaranteed the right to be secure from unreasonable arrest or detention and forbade arrest or detainer without a warrant unless probable cause existed. This proposal provided that evidence obtained in violation thereof would not be admissible in any civil or criminal proceeding.

BAIL AND HABEAS CORPUS

The report then concerned itself with the section in which bail and habeas corpus were conjoined. It noted the vote to make a minor change in punctuation but otherwise to retain unchanged section 7 of the 1870 bill of rights. There had been separate votes on the two clauses. The vote on the bail clause was 11 to 3 (with 1 absent). The vote on the habeas corpus clause was 9 to 3 (with 2 passing and 1 absent). The section read:

> *All persons shall be bailable by sufficient sureties, except for capital offenses where the proof is evident or the presumption great; and the privilege of the writ of* habeas corpus *shall not be suspended, unless when in cases of rebellion or invasion the public safety may require it.*

The report recounted that numerous suggestions were made for changes in both directions — towards increasing and towards decreasing liberality in release on bail. The committee opted for no change. It felt that Illinois was a leader in bail reform, and that the General Assembly could be relied on to consider further change.

It was pointed out that approximately half of the state bills of rights contained a provision similar to the Illinois section. Moreover, the Eighth Amendment to the federal constitution and the basic charters of the other states contained a provision prohibiting "excessive bail." Yet the principle was firmly established in Illinois by judicial decision.

As the report emphasized, some of the committee would have preferred language to clarify the limited purpose of bail and to promote the routine and regular release of persons accused of less serious offenses. Two proposals incorporated the ideas oriented in that more liberal direction. Two other proposals would have substituted the Eighth Amendment provision that "excessive bail shall not be required." Another proposal declared that all persons were bailable and that financial surety should be used only to assure their appearance at trial. One suggestion required that the General Assembly provide for a method of releasing accused persons upon their own recognizance where feasible, and provided for criminal penalties for violations by persons so released. After considerable debate, the committee rejected preventive detention for those accused of physical violence who had previously been convicted of such an offense and might commit violence if released.

The suggestion that "witnesses shall not be unreasonably detained" was rejected as merely restating the existing law in Illinois.

With respect to the second clause on habeas corpus, the committee saw no reason to change the existing language, identical to the language of the federal constitution and based on three-quarters of the state constitutions. This followed the suggestion of two member proposals.

The report pointed out that the provision was silent as to who could suspend the writ of habeas corpus in cases of rebellion or invasion, but that the power rested in the legislature and that governors in states with similar provisions have suspended the writ during public emergencies by declaring martial law and ordering military or other officials to detain persons without giving cause, and have been sustained by the courts.

Six committee members would have forbidden all suspensions of the writ of habeas corpus, unless permitted by judicial order after hearing, as it is provided in nine state constitutions. It was felt by the majority that some emergency powers ought to rest in the legislature.

INDICTMENT

The report then dealt with a subject of continuing interest — the manner in which to charge persons with offenses. The committee voted 12 to 3 to retain section 8 of the 1870 bill of rights unchanged except for a modification in the proviso:

No person shall be held to answer for a criminal offense, unless on indictment of a grand jury, except in cases in which the punish-ment is by fine, or imprisonment otherwise than in the penitentiary, in cases of impeachment, and in cases arising in the army and navy, or in the militia when in actual service in time of war or public danger: Provided, *that the grand jury may be abolished or its use limited in such cases as shall be determined by law.*

The new words, "or its use limited in such cases as shall be de-termined by law," were substituted for the 1870 proviso that the grand jury "may be abolished by law in all cases." This made ex-plicit what the Illinois Supreme Court had already held to be im-plicit — the General Assembly may abolish the grand jury in some or all situations. The report declared the section a satisfactory com-promise between an absolute requirement of grand jury indictment and a constitutional arrangement that would permit routine resort to prosecution by information filed by the prosecuting attorney. The provision was consonant with the Fifth Amendment to the United States Constitution and the constitutions of over forty states up to a point; but as in about a dozen states, the provision permitted aboli-tion of the ancient institution by law.

One proposal provided that persons could not be held to trial for any capital or other infamous crime other than by indictment. Two other proposals gave every person accused of a felony the right to require the prosecution to be originated by indictment, and not otherwise. They required a transcript of all grand jury proceedings and a prompt adversary preliminary hearing where the accused did not choose action by indictment.

There was much discussion, as the report emphasized, as to whether there should be preliminary hearings in all cases or only where there was no indictment, and whether there should be any grand jury action where there had been such preliminary hearing.

RIGHTS AFTER INDICTMENT

The report went on to a noncontroversial area — rights after indict-ment. It noted that the committee had voted 13 to 0 (with 2 absent) to retain unchanged section 9 of the 1870 bill of rights:

In all criminal prosecutions, the accused shall have the right to appear and defend in person and by counsel; to demand the nature and cause of the accusation, and to have a copy thereof; to meet the witnesses face to face, and to have process to compel the attendance of witnesses in his behalf, and a speedy public trial by an impartial jury of the county or district in which the offense is alleged to have been committed.

These were provisions contained in the constitutions of most states and were part of the basic guarantees of due process of law. The section was consonant with three proposals that the language be unchanged and one that would have substituted the language of the Sixth Amendment. Another proposal would have encompassed "any other proceeding wherein any person may be confined by virtue of State action for a period of 6 months or more."

SELF-INCRIMINATION AND DOUBLE JEOPARDY

The committee had voted 10 to 1 (with 4 absent) to retain unchanged section 10 of the 1870 bill of rights:

No person shall be compelled in any criminal case to give evidence against himself, or be twice put in jeopardy for the same offense.

The report was relatively brief dealing with self-incrimination and double jeopardy, already interpreted and clarified in numerous judicial decisions. There was fear that any change in language would cause uncertainty where once there was certainty.

The nine proposals considered by the committee would have left the clause as to self-incrimination unchanged or codified the substance of court decisions. The clear intent was expressed in one proposal: "No person shall be compelled to give evidence which might tend to incriminate him." It was felt that this was achieved through the old, often interpreted language.

Three proposals left the double jeopardy clause unchanged. Two proposals would have made substantive changes — forbidding a state prosecution of a defendant to whom jeopardy had attached for the same offense in the federal jurisdiction, and forbidding the putting of a defendant in jeopardy for the same offense in different jurisdictions of the state or its cities or other subdivisions.

LIMITATION OF PENALTIES AFTER CONVICTION

The report dealt with several proposals in the area of limitation of penalties, after noting that the committee had voted 7 to 5 (with 3 absent) to retain unchanged section 11 of the 1870 bill of rights:

> *All penalties shall be proportioned to the nature of the offense; and no conviction shall work corruption of blood or forfeiture of estate; nor shall any person be transported out of the state for any offense committed within the same.*

The point was not raised, but this vote was actually one less than a majority of the committee. A minority had wanted to express the rehabilitative purposes of punishment: "All penalties shall be proportioned both to the nature of the offense and to the objective of restoring the offender to useful citizenship."

Corruption of blood, forfeiture of estate, and transportation may be archaic forms of punishment, as the report said, but the committee was unanimous in continuing their prohibition in the bill of rights, as did many other state constitutions. Some would have augmented these ancient provisions by banning "permanent forfeiture of civil rights" or the "rights of citizenship."

Some rejected member proposals asked for omission of all or some of the provisions in the section. They would substitute the prohibition against cruel and unusual punishment of the Eighth Amendment of the federal constitution.

Three proposals, including one submitted by the chairman, would have abolished the death penalty. One proposal favored by the chairman would have automatically restored civil rights when a person convicted of a crime had served his term or had successfully completed parole. Another proposal would have required all penal institutions to conform to the health, safety, and security standards prescribed for comparable federal institutions. As the report said, the committee felt that these proposals and others, however meritorious, were appropriate for consideration by the General Assembly, but not for inclusion in the bill of rights. At least one proposal, rejected by the committee, would have restricted the authority of the courts and have yielded unduly to the harsh law-and-order line of some extremists.

IMPRISONMENT FOR DEBT

In imprisonment for debt, the report, like the committee, had much to discuss. But the committee voted 9 to 1 (with 2 passing and 3 absent) to retain unchanged section 12 of the 1870 bill of rights:

> *No person shall be imprisoned for debt, unless upon refusal to deliver up his estate for the benefit of his creditors, in such manner as shall be prescribed by law; or in cases where there is strong presumption of fraud.*

Because a number of committee members expressed dissatisfaction with the form and substance of the guarantee against imprisonment for debt, the report reviewed the effect of the 1870 provision.

The Illinois Supreme Court had held that section 12 only prohibited imprisonment for "judgments that arise out of contracts, either express or implied," so that the General Assembly could pass laws that require imprisonment of defendants unable to pay judgments in tort actions. The statutes sanctioned imprisonment for tort judgments when there was a special finding that "malice is the gist of the action" or "when the defendant shall refuse to deliver up his estate for the benefit of his creditors."[5] Nor would section 12 prevent a court from imprisoning persons for the nonpayment of money judgments stemming from equity decrees, including alimony payments, misuse of a trust fund, and failure to pay the rent awarded in a restitution decree. It would not prevent imprisoning the defendant in any civil case by a *capias ad respondendum* to assure his appearance at the trial, or for nonpayment of criminal fines.

After reviewing the many circumstances in which the 1870 provision did not forbid imprisonment for debt and considering many proposed changes, the committee concluded that it preferred the old language to any new alteration. Again it concluded that any reforms in this area should be left to the legislature. Among the rejected proposals was one forbidding imprisonment for failure to pay a fine in a criminal case unless the fine was set in accordance with the defendant's ability to pay, unless the defendant was afforded time to make payment, and unless he willfully failed to make payment.

[5] *Illinois Revised Statutes*, 1969, ch. 77, sec. 5.

Right of Eminent Domain

Again, in the area of the taking of private property, the report, like the committee, had much to say.

The committee voted 8 to 6 (with 1 absent) to substitute the following provision in place of section 13 of the 1870 bill of rights:

> *Private property shall not be taken, damaged, or the use thereof impaired, for public use, without just compensation to the full extent of the loss. Such compensation shall be determined by a jury, as shall be prescribed by law.*

The changes were substantial. They were intended to increase the number of public takings of property for which compensation must be paid, to enlarge the measure of damages, to broaden the circumstances in which the property owner had a right to a jury trial, and to eliminate the special treatment given for the fee of land taken for railroad tracks. The changes included the following:

(1) The old language referred to property being "taken or damaged." The revised section referred to property being "taken, damaged, *or the use thereof impaired*." In other words, it went beyond a mere taking or damaging, but it still encompassed "for public use," that is, public benefit. Still, it would not cover every instance in which police power was exercised in the interest of the health, safety, morals, or general welfare of the public and the use or value of property was affected. As heretofore, there would be no right to compensation for proper zoning laws or building code restrictions, even if they restricted the use and affected the value of property.

(2) Not alone "just compensation," but "just compensation *to the full extent of the loss*" would be required. There would be recovery for loss excluded under the old language, such as loss of business, moving costs, mortgage expenditures, or other deprivations because of condemnation.

(3) While the statutes granted a jury trial upon the demand of either party,[6] this was not a constitutional right so far as taking by the state was concerned. The revised section would give all parties a right to have compensation assessed by a jury in all cases.

(4) The amended section eliminated the special treatment that

---

[6] *Illinois Revised Statutes*, 1969, ch. 47, sec. 1.

the 1870 provision gave to lands taken for railroad purposes. The old provision prevented the taking of a so-called interest in fee, and made a reversion possible. The 1870 section limited a railroad to the acquisition of an easement, so that unless the landowner had voluntarily given the railroad a larger interest, the landowner would re-acquire the property if the railroad abandoned the route for any reason. This had complicated the process of getting and financing clear title for land under abandoned railroad tracks. The committee felt that railroads should be on the same footing as other bodies, governmental or private, that had the power of eminent domain. The situation could be governed by legislation, if necessary. Of course the change was not retroactive.

The report pointed out that the General Assembly would retain authority to make reasonable laws concerning the vesting of title, the procedure to be followed by the jury, and the time and manner in which compensation must be paid.

The revised section was based upon a consideration of at least nine member proposals, which it accepted or rejected, in whole or in part. The subject had elicited suggestions by special interest public bodies and several members representing public or private interests.

Ex Post Facto Laws, Impairing Contracts, and Sovereign Immunity

To an old section with time-honored language, the committee added something new. The report, like the committee, addressed itself briefly to the section.

The committee voted 13 to 0 (with 1 passing and 1 absent) to retain the language of section 14 of the 1870 bill of rights as the first sentence of the new provision, and voted 13 to 0 (with 2 absent) to add a new second sentence, the whole section reading:

> *No ex post facto law, or law impairing the obligation of contracts, or making any irrevocable grant of special privileges or immunities, shall be passed. The State shall have no special immunity from suit.*

The first sentence was old and noncontroversial. It was found in one form or another in about half of the state constitutions and was similar to the prohibition on state action in section 10 of Article I, of the federal constitution. There were two member proposals on the general subject matter.

The second sentence was new, far-reaching, and basic. It abolished sovereign immunity. It set aside Article IV, section 26, of the 1870 constitution, which provided: "The State of Illinois shall never be made defendant in any court of law or equity." But it was not intended to waive the immunity conferred on the state by the Eleventh Amendment to the federal constitution, providing that a state cannot be sued in a federal court by citizens of another state or of a foreign country.

As the report summed it up: "By abolishing sovereign immunity in the State of Illinois this sentence intends to assure that the State, all instrumentalities of the State, and all local government bodies will be subject to suit in the same manner as individual persons."

As the report demonstrated in detail, Illinois had been a leader in abolishing the immunity of local governmental units, as was evidenced by the famous *Molitor* case[7] and succeeding cases.

The report then attempted to show why the new provision did not affect the rules of law concerning the circumstances in which governmental entities or their employees would be liable for damages or other remedies, even though such rules might differ from the rules of liability pertaining to private individuals or corporations.

No purpose will be served here by a legislative discussion of the matter. Suffice it to say that there are areas in which governmental liability differs from individual or corporate liability, inherent in the nature and necessities of the varying situations. Thus, the new provision does not intend to upset the rules of liability prescribed in the Local Governmental and Governmental Employees Tort Immunity Act[8] or to prevent the enactment of similar legislation.

Other committees, at least the General Government Committee, had proposals on sovereign immunity, but there were no such proposals referred to the Bill of Rights Committee.

SUBORDINATION OF MILITARY POWER

Neither the report nor the committee devoted much time to the well-recognized principle of the subordination of military powers.

[7] *Molitor v. Kaneland Community School District,* 18 Ill. 2d 11 (1959).
[8] *Illinois Revised Statutes,* 1969, ch. 85, sec. 1–101 *et seq.*

The committee voted 14 to 0 (with 1 absent) to retain unchanged
section 15 of the 1870 bill of rights:

> *The military shall be in strict subordination to the civil power.*

This fundamental principle of American government was embodied in the constitutions of almost every state. No member submitted any proposal on the subject, and no alternatives were offered
in committee — something near a record.

QUARTERING OF SOLDIERS

The same was true of the quartering of soldiers.

The committee voted 14 to 0 (with 1 absent) to retain unchanged
section 16 of the 1870 bill of rights:

> *No soldier shall, in time of peace, be quartered in any house with-*
> *out the consent of the owner; nor in time of war except in the*
> *manner prescribed by law.*

This was practically identical to the Third Amendment to the
federal constitution. Again, no member submitted any proposals
on the subject, and no alternatives were offered in committee.

RIGHT TO ASSEMBLE AND PETITION

The report told the interesting story of what befell the old provision on the right to assemble. It was at first the story of the moun-
tain laboring and bringing forth a mouse.

The committee first voted 13 to 0 (with 2 absent) to insert a
comma after the word "manner," but otherwise to retain unchanged
section 17 of the 1870 bill of rights. Then, during deliberation on
a proposal concerning the right of free association introduced by
Father Lawlor, the committee voted 7 to 6 (with 2 absent, thus
less than a majority) to insert the words "to associate freely" following the word "manner." The version thus read as follows:

> *The people have the right to assemble in a peaceable manner, to*
> *associate freely, to consult for the common good, to make known*
> *their opinions to their representatives, and to apply for redress of*
> *grievances.*

As the report noted, virtually all state constitutions preserved the right to assemble and petition although in varying language. No other state provision was exactly like section 17 of the 1870 bill of rights, and none exactly like the proposed revision.

There was no little purpose in inserting the comma after "manner." It was to assure that the right to assemble in a peaceable manner was an independent right, unqualified by any of the succeeding phrases. Most state constitutions expressed the matter in the same way as the 1870 version of section 17, but seven states have made it an independent right. The section as approved made certain that people could assemble in a peaceable manner even if their purpose was other than "to consult for the common good, to make known their opinions to their representatives, and to apply for redress of grievances." The comma drew unanimous support.

The phrase "to associate freely" was inserted during a debate on a lengthy proposal by Father Lawlor which seemed to focus upon the area, but which the committee rejected. The resourceful Arthur Lennon, author earlier of the phrase "including the unborn" in the due process section, was likewise the creator of the effort to make Father Lawlor's proposal more palatable. This phrase was intended, in the committee's opinion, to reaffirm the principle of free association already implicit in the free speech guarantees of the federal and state constitutions. A substantial minority of the committee felt that the words were redundant at best and might have unintended adverse effects.

Three proposals considered by the committee either left the section unchanged or proposed minor revisions. One interesting proposal, supported by four members of the committee, provided a system of franking privileges for citizens to communicate with state officials.

ELECTIONS

Again, there was unanimity in the committee and little said in the report on free and equal elections.

The committee voted 14 to 0 (with 1 absent) to retain unchanged section 18 of the 1870 bill of rights:

All elections shall be free and equal.

The report noted that all state constitutions guaranteed free elections and almost twenty guaranteed "equal" elections.

One member proposal suggested that the section remain unchanged. Another proposal suggested the addition of these words: "The General Assembly shall make no law abridging the right to full and effective participation in political processes within the State of Illinois nor shall any law be administered by any public official in such manner as to abridge that right."

RIGHT TO REMEDY AND JUSTICE

Neither the report nor the committee agreed wholly with the chairman in assessing the effect of the revisions in the section on the right to a remedy.

The committee voted 11 to 4 to substitute the word "shall" for the words "ought to" in two places in section 19 of the 1870 bill of rights, and to retain the rest of the section unchanged:

> *Every person shall find a certain remedy in the laws for all injuries and wrongs which he may receive in his person, property or reputation; he shall obtain, by law, right and justice freely and without being obliged to purchase it, completely and without denial, promptly and without delay.*

This provision had similarities to those in most other state constitutions concerning redress for injuries, however much the precise language differed. The report stressed that the substitutions of "shall" for "ought to" were intended to make the principle more emphatic. It was suggested by four member proposals, one originated by the Chicago Bar Association. A few committee members felt the change was inappropriate; they wanted to retain the old language.

FUNDAMENTAL PRINCIPLES

The next section was not opposed. As the report pointed out, the committee voted 13 to 0 (with 1 passing and 1 absent) to retain unchanged section 20 of the 1870 bill of rights:

> *A frequent recurrence to the fundamental principles of civil government is absolutely necessary to preserve the blessings of liberty.*

There were similar provisions in about a dozen state constitutions. The provision was not substantive; it neither created nor diminished any rights. It was simply a "constitutional sermon," not really an operative part of the constitution. The committee felt that it was worth retaining the language for its teaching purpose.

One member proposal urged that the section remain unchanged. Another added a sentence directing that the people be given an opportunity to review such principles from time to time. Otherwise there was silence from the convention and the people.

RIGHTS RETAINED

Although new, the provision on rights retained was uncontested and noncontroversial. Neither the report nor the committee said much about it.

The committee voted 11 to 0 (with 4 absent) to add the following new provision to the bill of rights:

> *The enumeration in this Constitution of certain rights shall not be construed to deny or disparage others retained by the individual citizens of this State.*

As the reports said: "This provision gives explicit recognition to the principle that the Bill of Rights is not an exhaustive catalog of a citizen's rights and immunities in respect to government action."

It pointed out that the language was the same as the Ninth Amendment to the federal constitution, except that "people" has been replaced by "individual citizens of this State." The provision followed the one proposal submitted on the subject. Roy Pechous, not one of the activists of the committee, was the author.

DISCRIMINATION

The report dealt in considerable depth with what was probably the most basic matter in the new bill of rights — discrimination.

The committee voted 9 to 4 (with 2 absent) for the following new provision:

> *Every person shall have a right to freedom from discrimination on the basis of race, color, creed, national ancestry or sex in the*

hiring and promotion practices of any employer or in the sale or rental of property.

These rights shall be enforceable without action by the General Assembly, but the General Assembly may establish reasonable exemptions relating to these rights and may prescribe additional remedies for the violation of these rights.

With respect to discrimination by government, the provision simply supplemented the equal protection clause. As to private persons, important new rights were created. As the report said:

The Committee heard numerous witnesses and consulted many documents on the evil effects of discrimination on the basis of race, color, creed, national ancestry and sex. The Committee considered many different proposals for constitutional provisions to combat discrimination. Some were narrowly drawn to reach a single type of discrimination, such as discrimination against women in employment, and some were very broad and far-reaching, such as a proposal that would have even forbidden discrimination in voluntary associations. The Committee finally concluded that there should be a constitutional provision forbidding discrimination, and that the provision should be specifically directed at and limited to the important areas of employment and the sale or rental of property. The Committee resolved that the time had arrived when all persons subject to the laws of the State of Illinois should enjoy a constitutional right to freedom from discrimination by private persons as well as by public agencies in these important areas.

The report dealt with the kinds of reasonable exemptions that might be established by the legislature. To cite one example, it is of course proper for a congregation to utilize a religious test in employing a minister. There are other similar exemptions that are wholly proper.

It was realized that the propriety of particular reasonable exceptions could not readily be treated in a constitutional provision, but must be set forth by legislation.

The legislature was authorized to prescribe additional remedies for aggrieved persons. It could not take away any remedy, nor undermine the basic right, but it might, for example, protect women against the known hazards of certain kinds of employment.

The report explained why certain areas of discrimination were omitted from the section. They were either adequately covered by statute or court decisions, or not basic.

At this time, for the reasons noted by the report, no affirmative action was taken as to discrimination on the basis of physical or mental disability, the subject of one proposal. The committee thought that this was a matter for legislative rather than constitutional action.

The word "rental" as used in the section was meant to include leaseholds and all other arrangements by which the possession or use of property was exchanged for a valuable consideration; and "property" meant all property. For a variety of reasons relating to the areas of free choice and what is properly included in a constitution, some committee members opposed the provision.

The report contained a brief analysis of the constitutional provisions against discrimination in six state charters possibly reaching private as well as public discrimination. Four of these states — Alaska, Hawaii, Michigan, and New York — forbade discrimination in the enjoyment of "civil rights" or "civil and political rights." It was doubtful that this kind of provision created any independent right or remedy against discrimination. New York's court of appeals held that its provision did not outlaw racial discrimination in housing until implemented by legislation because "the civil rights protected by the clause in question were those already denominated as such in the constitution itself, in the Civil Rights Law or in other statutes."

Of the few other provisions in state constitutions briefly described in the report, none was as far-reaching as ours.

Many members of the convention submitted proposals on the topic of discrimination. The report enumerated these. One proposal was inspired by the Michigan Bill of Rights guaranteeing that no person would be denied the enjoyment or be discriminated against in the exercise "of his civil or political rights." Another proposal stated that "the right of the people to education, employment, housing, voluntary association and political participation" should not be infringed on the basis of race, creed, color, national origin, or sex. These and other proposals left uncertainty as to the meaning of the "rights." The committee preferred a provision with clear definition of the areas prescribed. It rejected some proposals that were definite enough but of possibly limited appeal, such as one forbidding discrimination against persons who had been arrested.

Preliminary Hearing

Just as the individual dignity section owed its adoption to Victor Arrigo, the preliminary hearing provision may be attributed to William Fennoy although the report, being impersonal, does not say so.

The committee voted 10 to 3 (with 2 passing) to add the following new section:

> *No person shall be held to answer for a crime punishable by death or imprisonment in the penitentiary without a prompt preliminary hearing to establish probable cause.*

The report told in explicit terms the current state of the law:

> Illinois law currently requires that a person who is arrested shall be taken before a judge "without unnecessary delay." The judge must inform the defendant of the charge against him, advise him of his right to counsel (and appoint counsel where appropriate), admit him to bail in accordance with law, and hold a preliminary hearing in those cases where the judge is without jurisdiction to try the offense. Ill. Rev. Stats., 1969, Ch. 38, Sec. 109–1. In practice the last requirement means that a preliminary hearing is required if an accused felon is brought before a magistrate (who has no jurisdiction to try a felony) but it is not required if he is brought before a circuit judge. In the preliminary hearing the judge determines whether "there is probable cause to believe an offense has been committed by the defendant." Illinois Rev. Stats., 1969, Ch. 38, Sec. 109–3.

The new section makes the often ignored statutory provisions mandatory. For one thing, it would make certain that an accused would have a right to preliminary hearing without regard to the jurisdiction of the judicial officer before whom he appeared and without regard to the manner of bringing the charge.

The accused is entitled to a judicial proceeding in which he may confront and cross-examine the witnesses who give evidence against him and may offer evidence in his own behalf.

The meaning of "prompt" is left to judicial construction in light of all the circumstances and other constitutional guarantees.

If the evidence does not show probable cause, the accused is entitled to be discharged. The report opined that the prosecution might bring new charges if more evidence should become available to establish probable cause.

Generally, the preliminary hearing will precede action by the grand jury, but it may follow such action occasionally. When the preliminary hearing is held after the indictment, it will serve the important purpose of requiring the prosecution to make public disclosure of sufficient evidence to furnish probable cause for holding the defendant to answer the charge. In the absence of probable cause, the judge should quash the indictment and discharge the defendant. Here, too, the report says that the prosecutor might bring new charges if more evidence should become available to establish probable cause.

The report sums up the matter: "As a constitutional principle, this provision is entirely new. Some states require preliminary examination before a person can be prosecuted for felony by information, but none has applied the principle to prosecutions by indictment, and comparatively few have chosen to make any mention of the preliminary hearing in their constitutions."

Public Employees

The report then dealt with the committee's effort to constitutionalize the rights of public employees. The committee voted 9 to 6 to add this new provision:

> *All public employees shall have the right to organize and bargain collectively. The General Assembly shall provide for the orderly exercise of this right.*

The report traced the history of the unionization of public employees as they grew in number (presently 10 percent of all employees in the state) and the responses of the courts. Court decisions have established important guiding principles. One federal appeals court had held that the First Amendment to the federal constitution guaranteed the right of public employees to form or join a union.

A state appellate court had held that the Chicago Board of Education might lawfully bargain and agree with an exclusive representative of its teachers. To resolve doubts on the subject, the committee decided to express its views in a constitutional provision.

The right of all public employees to organize or join a labor organization was affirmed, as was their right to engage in collective bargaining with their employer, and finally, the General Assembly was directed to provide for the orderly exercise of the right.

The committee was careful to point out that the new provision does not create a right to strike. There being all sorts of public employees with varying degrees of effect on the community, the subject of implementation was left to the General Assembly. Some would have preferred leaving the whole subject of public employees to the legislature.

The provision was unique in state constitutions. Two states, Hawaii and New Jersey, had constitutional provisions granting public employees "the right to organize, present to and make known to the State . . . their grievances and proposals through representatives of their own choosing." But the New Jersey Supreme Court had held that the provision did not give public employees the right to strike.

There were three member proposals considered by the committee in this area, one even permitting concerted action, but in the end the committee resolved the matter through the proposed new section, leaving all else to the legislature.

Basic Needs

The report devoted little space to an entirely new section on basic needs of the individual.

The committee voted 8 to 7, a bare majority, with all members voting, to add the following new provision to the bill of rights:

> *It shall be the public policy of the state that all persons shall have adequate nourishment, housing, medical care and other needs of human life and dignity.*

Again, the report stressed the hortatory nature of the provision, its lack of operative effect. This was the one provision proposed by

Albert Raby that survived committee deliberations, thanks to un-expected support from the usually conservative Arthur Lennon. The report mentioned that there were no comparable provisions in any other state constitutions.

Some committee members contended that the government dis-charged any responsibility by providing for education and nondis-criminatory employment, and thus allowing citizens to take care of these essentials for themselves. Other members objected to the pro-liferation of hortatory statements in the bill of rights.

One proposal of the same genre as the one adopted would have "insured" as an inherent and inalienable right of every individual the availability of adequate nourishment, shelter, clothing, and medical care. Another proposal declared that health was a basic human right for every citizen and that it was the responsibility of government to enable all citizens to secure quality health care re-gardless of ability to pay.

INDIVIDUAL DIGNITY

Considering the novel and controversial nature of the concept of individual dignity, the report was unusually brief in its presentation.

The committee voted 9 to 4 (with 2, including the chairman, passing) to add the following new provision to the bill of rights:

> *To promote the dignity of the individual, communications that portray criminality, depravity or lack of virtue in or that incite violence, hatred, abuse or hostility toward any group of persons in this State by reason of or by reference to religious, racial, ethnic or national affiliation are condemned.*

As the report summed it up:

> This provision seeks to encourage moderation in the use of lan-guage that impairs the dignity of individuals by disparaging groups to which they belong. It in no way qualifies or modifies the con-stitutional rights of free speech and press. The provision creates no private right or cause of action, and it imposes no limitation on the powers of Government.

Again, there was the language about a "constitutional sermon." This provision was the brain child of Victor Arrigo. There were no other member proposals on this question, and there was no comparable provision in any other state constitution. Without Arrigo, it would not have passed; without him, it would not have been proposed. As the report said:

> The Committee members who opposed this provision were of the view that it could result in discouraging complete freedom of expression, even if it did not qualify or modify the right of free speech and press in any formal sense. They also maintained that, apart from the merits of the proposal, this is not the kind of subject that is appropriately treated in a Constitution.

RIGHT TO ARMS

The report left for the last the highly controversial right to arms. It devoted more attention to this subject than any other.

The committee voted 12 to 3 to add the following new provision:

> *Subject only to the police powers of the State, the right of the individual citizen to keep and bear arms shall not be infringed.*

How far does the right extend? What are the limitations required by the safety and good order of society? The report sought to place the provision in perspective by reviewing other comparable constitutional provisions, and the cases construing them.

The Second Amendment to the federal constitution provides:

> A well regulated Militia, being necessary to the security of a free State, the right of the people to keep and bear Arms, shall not be infringed.

It appeared from the interpretations by the United States and Illinois Supreme Courts that the Second Amendment language referred only to a collective right, reasonably connected to the maintenance of a militia or other form of common defense, and not to any individual right to bear arms.

Thirty-five state constitutions had provisions concerning the right to keep or bear arms. At least eleven of these seemed limited to a collective right, rather than an individual right to bear arms. Eleven constitutions declared an individual right to bear arms. Thirteen states had provisions that were unclear on whether the right to arms was only a collective right, for the common defense, or whether it also guaranteed a right to the individual. Some leaned one way, some another.

By thus referring to "the individual citizen" and to the right to "keep" as well as to "bear" arms, the proposed new Illinois provision guaranteed an individual right rather than a collective right. The citizen was given the right to possess and make reasonable use of arms that law-abiding persons commonly employ for purposes of recreation or the protection of person and property. *All* possession or use of such arms could not be banned by law or subjected to taxes so onerous that all possession or use was banned in effect.

But what does the police power entail? In the earliest decision on the permissible regulatory power concerning firearms, the Illinois Supreme Court upheld the validity of a Chicago ordinance that required that all sellers and buyers of pistols obtain a license. The court said that under the police power the sale of all deadly weapons might be banned. More recently, the state supreme court cited the early case with approval in an opinion upholding the validity of the Chicago gun registration ordinance.

Here are some regulatory measures that have been approved by courts as not constituting an unconstitutional infringement of even an individual right to arms:

(1) The state may prohibit altogether the possession of certain deadly weapons not commonly and peacefully used by individuals, such as machine guns, firearms equipped with silencing devices, gas-ejecting devices, blackjacks, artillery weapons, bombs, and so forth.

(2) The state may forbid or regulate the possession or use of firearms by minors or by persons whose physical or mental disabilities or violent propensities shown by prior criminal conduct present unacceptable risks of danger to themselves or others. For this purpose the state may adopt a reasonable licensing law pertaining to those who possess or use firearms, and Illinois and many states have done so.

(3) The state may prohibit or regulate the carrying of *concealed* weapons, and may enforce this power by licensing laws.

(4) In seeming contradiction of the above, the state may regulate or prohibit the carrying of weapons *openly* when there is no

good reason for such action and the regulation bears a fair relation to the preservation of public peace and safety.

(5) The state may regulate the purchase and sale of weapons, even to the extent of totally prohibiting the sale of some weapons in some circumstances.

These powers must be related to the public good, and must be consistent with other bill of rights guarantees, such as due process and equal protection of the laws.

States and other instrumentalities of government inherently have the rights indicated under their police power, but often make matters doubly certain by specific laws and constitutional provisions. The fact that the General Assembly has enacted regulatory laws does not prevent municipalities from doing so.

The provision resembled a member proposal providing that the right of the individual citizen to keep and bear arms should not be infringed except for the mentally ill or convicted felons. Four proposals sought to prevent registration and other controls, some going to great length to constitutionalize an individual right to keep and bear arms. In the other direction, one proposal used the Second Amendment language: "The right of the people to keep and bear arms shall not be infringed." Another proposal, introduced by the chairman but fathered by the Welfare Council of Metropolitan Chicago, urged that the bill of rights should contain no provision on the subject of arms, but should instead leave the subject to legislation.

Very briefly, the report summed up the view of the minority — Gertz, Raby, and Weisberg — who opposed the majority view. In due course, their views will be set forth in greater detail, as will the views of the respective minorities on other provisions.

V

The Minorities File Their Dissents

The chairman was later to stress on the floor of the convention how much agreement there was, in the end, on so many controversial issues. This may have arisen out of a sense of relief that the battles, in their committee phase at least, were at an end. When the committee report was assembled for presentation to the convention and the minority reports were put in shape, one might have been forgiven a degree of skepticism as to there being agreement on any level. Before there could be a minority report, three members had to join in it, according to the rules of the convention. This did not preclude any member from opposing any part of any report on the floor of the convention and offering amendments galore. Some committees had a sense of *esprit de corps* about uniting in support of their product. The Bill of Rights Committee had great pride in its work, but no member felt that he was bound in any way. Indeed, in the introductory pages of the report it was stated that signing it was simply an act of certification of genuineness, rather than an approval of contents. At the end of the convention a similar formula for signing was voted by the convention.

Foster, Dvorak, Lennon, and Pechous took strong exception to the new preamble, but they expressed themselves rather mildly in the very brief minority report they filed; one could not have recalled from it the acrimony of much of the committee discussion on the matter. The minority report read in full:

The Minority agrees with the principles expressed in the excellent proposal presented by Miss Odas Nicholson, Secretary of the Convention, and adopted by the Majority. We believe, however, that the principles of elimination of poverty and provision for protection and development of the individual can be added to the Preamble without losing the historical resonance of the present language. We further have strong reservations as to the possible legal effect of the language adopted by the Majority.

It immediately becomes apparent upon a quick perusal of the various minority reports — in all, there were ten of them — that those which originated in the more conservative bloc of the committee were quite brief, either out of a desire to get to the point at once or because they were taken less seriously than the civil libertarian group took their dissents. For the most part, in these ensuing pages the minority reports of the more conservative members are quoted in full while the other reports are largely paraphrased.

Pechous, who had joined one group in the first minority report, now joined another group in the minority report opposing the addition of the words, "including the unborn," in the due process clause. This was illustrative of how forces switched in the committee and at the convention. Few delegates were completely predictable in their reactions. In this instance the minority group included Gertz, Raby, Weisberg, and Wilson, besides Pechous. It should have included Foster, who had voted with us on the section, but he did not like the manner in which we expressed our dissent. Wilson was a sort of swing man on this and on several other issues. Conservative in bearing, he had strong views on certain human issues and would not hesitate to join with other individuals, no matter who they were, if they shared his views. On the other hand, Gertz, Raby, and Weisberg, civil libertarian to the core, almost invariably voted together on the more controversial issues that came before the convention. Sometimes they were alone in signing minority reports. Their singularity did not invariably mean defeat on the floor of the convention, as we shall see.

It is worth exploring the alignments further.

Wilson joined in the minority reports in opposition to the phrase "including the unborn," in opposition to the language about truth in libels, in opposition to constitutionalizing the rights of public employees, and in opposition to the section on individual dignity.

In two of these instances he was joined by Gertz, Raby, and Weisberg and in an additional one by Raby and Weisberg, so that only once — with respect to public employees — was he, the conservative, not allied with members of the liberal and independent bloc. Pechous joined with him in one minority report — in connection with the due process section — and Foster in connection with a minority report relating to individual dignity.

Lennon joined in four minority reports — against the revised preamble, against the revision of the eminent domain section, against the preliminary hearing section, and against constitutionalizing the rights of public employees. He was consistently conservative in his dissents. His colleagues in dissent could well have been anticipated — Hutmacher in three instances, Kelleghan, Pechous, Mrs. Macdonald, Dvorak, and Foster in other instances. Undoubtedly, Kelleghan would have been allied with Lennon more often had he been present when the minority reports were prepared.

To jump ahead of our narrative, how did the minority reports fare on the floor of the convention? Five of them won in whole or in part — the dissents as to the phrase "including the unborn," as to the eminent domain section, certain aspects of the preliminary hearing, public employees, and fines. Six of them lost in whole or in part — the dissents as to the preamble, truth in libel, certain aspects of the preliminary hearing, individual dignity, right to arms, and bail.

All things considered, this record is by no means a bad one, and it becomes better when one recalls the amendments to various sections from the floor and even the addition of two entire sections, as we shall see. It is clear that neither in the committee sessions nor on the floor of the convention, whether on first, second, or final readings, was anything a foregone conclusion so far as the bill of rights was concerned.

Was this any different from what befell other articles of the constitution? We shall observe a significant development in the attitude of the delegates towards the committee. It will be best to discuss this later when all of the facts are in.

Gertz, Raby, Weisberg, and Wilson commented in their minority report on the proposed due process clause (the first part of section 2):

The objection of the minority is directed solely to the inclusion of the words "including the unborn" in the due process clause of this section.

It is our position that the chief, if indeed not the only, effect of these words is to prohibit the General Assembly from enacting any laws to permit abortions, except presumably abortions which are now permitted under Illinois law where necessary to preserve the life of the mother. It seems clear that this has to be the effect if the words in question are to be given any significance whatsoever.

Although the majority disclaims any purpose to prohibit or restrict the enactment of laws relating to abortion, it is significant that some Committee members who spoke in support of these words [we might have mentioned Father Lawlor, for one] addressed themselves squarely to the question of abortion and favored these words because they would prohibit enactment of legislation legalizing abortion except in the limited situations noted above. We believe there is no lack of understanding in the Committee as to the real effect and intent of these words, and that the issue they present must be squarely faced.

It is the minority's position that the subject of abortion law should be left to the legislature, which can study and evaluate the pertinent medical and social facts and policy consideration.

We then devoted our attention to further support for our belief that the subject should be left to the General Assembly. We told of the increasing concern expressed in recent years about the effects of restrictive abortion laws. Such laws, we said, are ignored constantly by women wishing to end unwanted pregnancies, perhaps as many as 1,500,000 throughout the country. This inevitably leads to death and disease, as abortions which occur in such circumstances are performed by the least qualified rather than the most and in dreadful conditions. Those with financial means can do what is forbidden to the less prosperous.

We discussed the kinds of laws that had been passed, liberalizing the grounds for abortion, and the good reasons for such laws, highly recommended by reputable persons and agencies. We expressed the opinion that every woman has a basic personal right to determine when and whether to bear children. We told of the defects of laws like those in force in Illinois, which were much too vague and interfere unduly with the right of physicians to practice their calling.

We reminded the convention that similar laws had been held unconstitutional recently. Various states, we said, had enacted more sensible laws than those currently in force and these ought to be emulated; at least the door ought not to be shut by the proposal of the majority of the committee, unprecedented in any state or federal constitution.

We pointed out that "unborn persons" was not defined, and that, read literally, the term would include not only fetuses but persons not yet conceived and would thus be federally unconstitutional. Bitingly, we opined that if the convention should decide that abortions ought to be dealt with in the constitution, this should be done directly, and not through any dodge.

We told of the deep religious differences on the issue, and declared that it would be wrong to constitutionalize the views of any group. We should be neutral and protect the rights of all persons to act in accordance with their own religious and moral convictions. We suggested that to do otherwise would jeopardize approval of the constitution.

The same four members of the committee filed a minority report in opposition to the final clause of the section on freedom of speech: ". . . and in all trials for libel, both civil and criminal, the truth, when published with good motives and for justifiable ends, shall be a sufficient defense." We expressed the belief that the words should either be omitted entirely, as recommended by the Chicago Bar Association and others, or that the words should be confined to "private matters."

We discussed at great length what the Illinois Supreme Court had said in the recent *Farnsworth* case, in which the committee chairman, now joining in the minority report, was losing counsel. We took up the *Farnsworth* opinion in detail, particularly the words:

> It is therefore clear that the Article II, Section 4 provisions of the Illinois Constitution that truth is a defense in a libel action only when published with good motives and for justifiable ends (*Ogren v. Rockford Star Printing Co.*, 288 Ill. 405), when applied to defamation of "public officials" or "public figures," is incompatible with the Supreme Court's interpretation of the scope of the first amendment guarantees of the Federal Constitution. *Accordingly,*

if the plaintiff is a "public figure" or if, as hereinafter discussed, the articles contain matters of public interest and concern so that the Federal Constitution safeguards apply, the trial court was correct in refusing to give the plaintiff's instruction based upon section 4 of article II.

We therefore conclude that the trial court correctly refused the plaintiff's instruction based upon the language contained in Section 4 of Article II of the Illinois Constitution *for that provision is federally unconstitutional as we have heretofore noted, to the extent that it would require a defendant who had published statements about public affairs or of public interest and concern to prove that they were true, and published with good motives and for justifiable ends.* It follows from this discussion that it was not error to give defendants' instructions. (Emphasis supplied)

We expressed our belief that the convention had the obligation to accept and conform to this authoritative declaration of the highest court of our state.

Then as to the *eminent domain* section, a minority, consisting of Dvorak, Hutmacher, Lennon, Pechous, and Father Lawlor, proposed to delete the concept of "impaired use" and the so-called "full extent of the loss." They declared:

"Impaired use" is vague, remote, incapable of reasonable definition and no one knows whether this requires the "condemnation" of all possible remote interests, or whether it is intended to give rise to a cause of action for damages in more or less remote types of inconvenience.

In any event, the measure and extent of damages is a more proper subject for the legislature and the common law decisions.

It is believed that the Majority recommended a change in this Section because of dissatisfaction with various statutory and legislative enactments relating to urban renewal, highway construction and other similar programs. These ills cannot be cured by constitutional change expanding "damages" because they go basically to a question of "necessity" for the taking, and whether the taking is, in fact, for a "public use."

The Minority agrees, however, that the railroad track provision of [this] section should be deleted.

Hutmacher, Kelleghan, and Lennon urged in a minority report the deletion of the section on preliminary hearing. They felt that this was a matter for legislative consideration and that the existing laws were adequate. They said:

"Held to answer" means called upon to plead guilty or not guilty. Since the only question before a grand jury is "probable cause" and since the preliminary hearing *also* decides "probable cause," the Majority proposal requires a duplication of the same finding. In other words, any prosecution for serious crime requires both the grand jury *and* a judge to find probable cause before being "held to answer."

In any event, if the Convention wants to retain the grand jury a "probable cause" preliminary hearing ought not duplicate the grand jury effort.

If the grand jury is constitutionally important, then the legislature ought not be able to deny it, as the Majority would allow. Conversely, if the grand jury is not constitutionally important, then it should be replaced by an alternate procedure (such as the State's Attorney filing an "information" followed by a preliminary hearing). In either event there is little if any sound reason to require two procedures which require the same decision to be made by separate bodies. . . .

On public employees, Hutmacher, Lennon, Wilson, and Mrs. Macdonald expressed in a minority report their belief that the testimony before the committee overwhelmingly advised constitutional silence on the subject of labor-management relations including right to work, collective bargaining, and so forth. They gave several reasons why this provision should not be added:

(1) The equal protection clause of the 14th amendment of the Federal Constitution adequately protects public employees.

(2) This added clause may impair the functions of the two party system in this State by restricting or prohibiting a change of personnel in government following an election.

(3) The entire subject is so complex including as it does, the establishment of bargaining procedures, remedies, the right to strike or take other concerted action, that it should be left to the General Assembly to work out in detail.

(4) The provision is unnecessary as the courts have already recognized the right of public employees in Illinois to organize and bargain collectively.

They were succinct, if not cogent, in their categorically expressed views.

A different sort of minority — Foster, Raby, Weisberg, and Wilson (the chairman, usually allied with Raby and Weisberg, had passed) — opposed the new individual dignity section. They said they "do not condone or approve communications that disparage groups of people on the ground of religion, race or ethnic or national affiliation. They feel just as strongly as do the majority that such comments are in extremely bad taste, to say the least, and they sympathize with those against whom the remarks are directed. However, it does not follow that the Constitution should therefore include a provision against this kind of thing."

They analyzed the testimony of the five witnesses who had appeared before the committee and observed: "We do not believe that the general public regards all Italians or those of Italian ancestry as criminals or having criminal tendencies, any more than it believes all Irishmen to be drunkards or all Englishmen to be smug and conceited, and so on down the line."

They cautioned about the need for "a careful and exhaustive review and appraisal of evidence, statistical and otherwise, submitted by representatives of a great many of the different groups affected by such remarks." They said that this was a legislative matter, not something for a constitutional convention. "It is not the proper function of a Constitution to deal with every meritorious cause or to prescribe a remedy for every complaint, even if well taken." Maligned individuals, they said, have "full recourse under the laws of Illinois covering libel and slander."

They objected to the hortatory nature of the section, saying that "in no case should such statements be expanded to cover subjects not previously included."

Finally, they expressed fear as to the effect on freedom of speech, despite assurances to the contrary.

Only Gertz, Raby, and Weisberg joined in the remaining three minority reports — on the right to arms, bail, and imprisonment for debt. While all three took responsibility for the reports, Weisberg was almost exclusively responsible for the language.

All three of us felt that it was unwise and dangerous to add a new provision to the Illinois Constitution creating an individual right to keep and bear arms. We felt the majority section was so ambiguous and self-contradictory that its meaning and effect could not be determined even by lawyers. We thought that it created uncertainty about the power of the legislature to enact gun control laws needed in the interest of public safety. We felt that serious public misunderstanding and litigation would be involved. In the end it would lead to a more stringent federal system of handgun licensing.

"In view of the extraordinary threat to public safety posed by firearms, the Convention has a heavy responsibility not to recommend constitutional restrictions which might handicap the legislature in protecting the public," we said. "This is especially important in view of the huge supply of firearms in private hands in the United States and the alarming increases in recent years in homicides, attacks on police and other crimes usually committed with guns."

The dissenters suggested that it was difficult to determine the meaning and effect of the committee proposal. What was this undefined individual right to keep and bear arms? In what manner was it subject to the vague concept of the "police powers"? We were troubled by the silences as to what new limits, if any, there would be on the power of the legislature to enact various undescribed types of gun control laws in order to cope with any emergency.

We felt that the majority proposal would add nothing to the existing requirement that any gun control legislation must meet constitutional standards of reasonableness, so that the proposed constitutional change was a meaningless act, only adding to the ambiguity of the prevailing situation. The proposal might defeat its very purpose by bringing federal legislation and a preemption in this important area. By wanting too much, the majority might get too little. "The general public cannot be expected to understand," we said, "that since the proposed individual constitutional right is completely subordinate to the 'police power' of the state, the 'right' may turn out to be without content. This type of constitutional change is not likely to build public confidence in the work of the Convention."

We traced the history of the struggle against firearms, particularly the efforts of J. Edgar Hoover and others to secure more effective gun control. We showed how the mere presence of guns means that they will be used; that the homicide rate will go up as a matter of course. We cited statistics to prove our point. We tried to be as rational as possible. Then we summed up as fervently as possible:

> In recent years the rhetoric of extremist groups urging their followers to arm themselves, together with fear of civil disorders, has contributed to a climate in which discussion of firearms legislation frequently becomes highly charged emotional debate. The Convention must seek to avoid such debate and focus instead on its responsibility to generations to come, whose problems in this field may be even more serious than ours.
>
> The proposed right to bear arms is without precedent in the Illinois Constitution. The report of the Committee mentions no reason whatever for adding a provision of this kind at this time. No need has been shown for constitutional change on this subject.
>
> In our climate of concern about violence, a new constitutional right to bear arms is not the ethical message needed by the people of our State and our nation.

Once more the minority of Gertz, Raby, and Weisberg differed with the majority of the committee; this time with respect to the bail clause of section 7. We proposed the following revision: "All persons shall be bailable, except for capital offenses where the proof is evident or the presumption great. Security shall be required only to assure the appearance of the accused and shall not exceed the financial means of the accused."

We declared: "The money bail system leads each year to the jailing, solely because of their poverty, of thousands of defendants awaiting trial. These defendants are not only punished without a trial or conviction; they are also handicapped in preparing their defense." These practices, we said, have been condemned by two presidential commissions and lead to the feeling, among the poor, that "lower courts in our urban communities dispense 'assembly line' justice; that from arrest to sentencing, the poor and uneducated are denied equal justice with the affluent, that procedures such as bail and fines have been perverted to perpetuate class inequities."[1]

Pretrial release on bail is fundamental to our system of criminal

[1] National Advisory Commission on Civil Disorders, *Report* (Washington, D.C.: U.S. Government Printing Office, 1968), p. 183.

justice. It prevents punishment prior to conviction and gives the opportunity for adequate preparation. Securing the appearance of the accused is the sole function of bail. The minority proposal would have left the courts with ample powers to deal with those defendants who might flee or engage in criminal conduct before trial.

We were not unaware that in 1963 Illinois adopted model bail reform legislation, providing for the setting of bail according to the circumstances of each case.[2] The statute requires that the amount of bail should not be oppressive and should be considerate of the financial ability of the accused. It provided for the liberal use of release on personal recognizance. But in practice, the statute had not really solved the most serious problems, which the minority report enumerated:

(1) Each year, thousands of defendants are confined in Illinois jails awaiting trial solely because they, unlike other defendants charged with similar crimes and for whom similar bail amounts have been fixed, are too poor to deposit the amount of money required to obtain pretrial release. [This we documented from studies made of the bail situation in Illinois.]

(2) Such jailing involves punishment without trial or conviction of a crime. Jailing is called "punishment" after conviction, but is called "security for appearance" before. Yet they have the same effect upon the accused. [This is especially offensive where the accused is in the end not convicted of any offense, true in 18 to 67 percent of the cases.]

(3) Many economic and social costs result from confining persons awaiting trial. There is a financial burden upon the accused and his family, for he loses his job and his pay for the duration of the confinement and trial. Such imprisonment costs taxpayers millions of dollars per year.

(4) The denial of pretrial release affects the fairness of the defendant's trial. The defendant who is jailed is handicapped in preparing his defense, is more likely to be convicted, is more likely to receive a longer sentence and is less likely to be considered for probation than similar defendants who obtained pretrial release.

(5) High bail is frequently set for the improper purpose of inflicting punishment before trial or confining persons who it is feared will commit crimes if released before trial.

[2] *Illinois Revised Statutes,* 1969, ch. 38, sec. 110.

The minority revision would have accomplished the following:

(1) It would have emphasized the impropriety of fixing high bail to make it impossible for the defendant to obtain pretrial release.

(2) It would have eliminated as unnecessary the reference to sureties in the 1870 section, since bail bondsmen had been abolished by statute. Where security was required, there could be a deposit of money equal to 10 percent of the bail or a deposit of securities or real estate.

(3) Since no defendant was to be confined solely because of his poverty, bail, where necessary, would have to be fixed within the defendant's ability to secure, if necessary, in installments.

(4) As to convicted defendants, bail pending appeal was left to the legislature.

We stressed that the only objection to our proposal and to the total abolition of money bail was the need to deal with the "small percentage of defendants who present a significant risk of flight or criminal conduct before trial."[3] Our proposal would not have disturbed the ample powers of the courts for dealing with such persons.

First, it was clear that present bail practices did not deal effectively with defendants likely to flee in a manner fair to defendants who present no such risk. "Bail is typically fixed in accordance with a standard schedule of bail amounts believed appropriate to the type of crime charged and without consideration of the defendant's employment record, family ties and other circumstances which must be evaluated to make a fair determination whether he is likely to appear for trial." There were no obstacles to professional criminals; they, the most dangerous, could easily post bond.

Second, only a small percentage of accused persons failed to appear for trial. Many bond forfeitures were caused by confusion over the trial date and not through flight. Financial incentives would probably be the least effective means of assuring appearance for trial.

"Third, as to the defendant believed to be dangerous, no method has been proved to be reliable for predicting whether any particular person is likely to commit any particular type of crime if released to await trial."

[3] President's Commission on Law Enforcement and Administration of Justice, *Task Force Report* (Washington, D.C.: U.S. Government Printing Office, 1967), p. 131.

"Fourth, modern bail studies have stressed the availability of alternative methods to deal with cases in which the defendant may present a significant danger of criminal conduct before trial:"

(1) Accelerated trials for presumably high-risk defendants, and revoking of bail where the defendant delays trial unreasonably.

(2) The use of conditions and restrictions short of detention, such as periodically reporting to the police, a probation officer, or the court; curfews or restrictions on travel, association or place of residence; day-time release, allowing the defendant to continue his employment.

(3) Vigorous use of criminal punishment for violation of the conditions of the court's pretrial release order.

In a final minority report, Gertz, Raby, and Weisberg suggested that these words be added to the section on imprisonment for debt: "No person shall be imprisoned for failure to pay a fine in any criminal case unless the fine has been set in accordance with the defendant's financial means, the defendant has been afforded adequate time to make payment, in installments if necessary, and defendant has wilfully failed to make such payment."

Our proposal, we said, was intended to end the practice under which poor defendants convicted of an offense and fined were imprisoned because of their poverty, while financially able defendants in similar cases could pay their fines and go free. We referred to the large number of individuals confined in county jails for inability to pay their fines.

"Such imprisonment is discriminatory," we said. "It is also expensive to the community as well as the offender and his family. The ability of the wealthy defendant to avoid any imprisonment in contrast to the defendant who is jailed because of his poverty reinforces the view, found especially among the poor, that our legal system does not afford equal justice." We spelled out the costs to the community and showed how our proposal would lessen such costs and be more effective as a means of collecting fines.

Were we soft on crime, as some charged whenever an enlightened proposal was made? We answered this question, we thought, when we said: "Where a fine is the appropriate punishment, the court should punish the wealthy offender if he wilfully refuses to obey the order to pay, and it should employ flexible collection techniques for the poor to make payment possible. On the other hand, if the court really wishes to sentence the defendant to imprisonment, it should do so directly and avoid the impression that harsher imprisonment is given to the poor than to financially able defendants."

We showed from the New York City experience and what had happened in at least fourteen other states how much more in fines would be collected if our proposal was accepted. Even such conservative groups as the American Bar Association and the American Law Institute favored our plan. They agreed that the increased costs of administration would be more than offset by the greatly increased collections of fines.

We concluded: "The minority proposal would improve the fairness of our criminal justice system and increase respect for law throughout the community."

Thus the various issues were placed firmly before the convention in majority and minority reports.

VI

The Convention Disposes and Decrees

As Edward S. Gilbreth phrased it in the *Chicago Daily News* at
the beginning of June 1970, battle lines were being formed at the
convention as the long-awaited bill of rights report was about to
come up for consideration on first reading.[1] Our committee, as Gilbreth said, had "wrestled" with the "hottest issues." Now the convention as a whole would face the day of judgment on such basic
matters as abortion, gun control, the death penalty, free speech,
rights of privacy, search and seizure, and eminent domain, not to say
such other explosive matters as nondiscrimination, preliminary hearings for those accused of felonies, a new preamble — the inventory
of fireworks was almost inexhaustible. There were twenty-seven proposed sections, the preamble, and ten minority reports. How long
would it take the convention to battle its way through the agenda?
The optimists, according to Gilbreth's soundings, were saying two
weeks; the pessimists a month. And the convention could not really
spare that time. President Witwer was constantly reminding us that
we were a month behind schedule. There were rumors of deals between downstate delegates and Cook County Democrats, between
this group and that, on various proposals. Even deals could not stop
oratory under the generous rules of the convention. When the rules
were originally submitted to the convention for a vote, they had
been even more generous in the amount of time permitted each

[1] Edward S. Gilbreth, "Con-Con forms battle lines on rights bill," *Chicago
Daily News,* June 1, 1970.

delegate for speech-making. I had made the successful motion lopping off five minutes from the proposed time allotment. As time had gone on, I had regretted that I had not attempted to reduce the time further. Of course, I favored full debate, but I felt that the orators — of whom we had a God's plenty, including one of His priests — could learn to be less prolix; they could say more in less time.

Victor Arrigo gave a foretaste of what was to come even before his individual dignity section was presented. There was a proposal to delete mention of the World's Columbian Exposition of 1893 from the new constitution. Of course everyone including Arrigo knew that the provision was no longer necessary. It had fulfilled its function, and even those many like Kelleghan, who found each word and phrase of the 1870 language sacred and immutable, were reconciled to its disappearance from the basic charter. Arrigo organized a mock protest in which he drew in virtually all of the delegates as honorary Italians, protesting all affronts to that noble race of descendants of the Romans. He declared that removing the provision would give support to "scurrilous claims" that Columbus was not the true discoverer of America. For fifty-five minutes, by the solemnly moving clock, Arrigo recited the valorous deeds of gallant Italians, and twenty (presumably of Italian descent) momentarily passed their votes in protest against kissing off the Columbian Exposition. Thomas J. McCracken, almost every discerning person's favorite Daley Democrat, consoled Arrigo that "none of us are anti-Columbian, although in political philosophy some of us are accused of being pre-Columbian."

Thus was the stage set for the debate to come on individual dignity, with further flurries when anyone was so unwise as to refer to the Latins, Romans, Italians, Sicilians, or other designations noble or ignoble of Arrigo's proud ethnic group. Once a clergyman, in his invocation to the convention, dared refer disparagingly to some specimens of the Italian group. That meant more Arrigo oratory, and one could be sure that it would be stored up for the ultimate perorations.

On May 22, 1970, the report of the Bill of Rights Committee, its proposal 1, was formally presented to the convention. One week later, on May 29, the first action with respect to it was taken by the convention in committee of the whole. After the chairman and some of the members of the committee had outlined various sections and answered questions from the floor, President Witwer asked that some of the less controversial sections be voted on. Although this was contrary to the procedure that the committee had insisted on, I acquiesced. Five sections with no changes from the 1870 constitution were approved — section 1 (inherent and inalienable rights), section 3 (religious freedom), section 15 (subordination of military power), section 16 (quartering of soldiers), and section 18 (free and equal elections). No section on which any delegate raised a question or suggested the consideration of amendments was voted on. Then the convention recessed for the weekend.

On June 2, consideration of the bill of rights resumed. Six sections were approved, in some instances with amendments and in other instances without change. Section 4 (freedom of speech) was approved with the old clause on truth as defense in libel actions. Section 5 (trial by jury) was approved after being amended to provide that the General Assembly may authorize juries of not less than six nor more than twelve. Lewis Wilson had proposed the amendment, largely on the recommendation of Chief Justice Underwood of the Illinois Supreme Court. Section 9 (rights after indictment) and section 10 (protection against self-incrimination) were approved as submitted. Section 11 (limitation of penalties) was amended on motion of Leonard Foster to add the previously considered objective of rehabilitation of offenders, and then approved after the defeat, 54 to 50, of an amendment to prohibit the death penalty. Section 20 (fundamental principles of civil government) was approved after the addition of a statement on individual responsibility proposed by Dwight Friedrich, previously defeated in committee.

The next day, June 3, five more sections were approved on first reading: section 8 (indictments), section 14 (ex post facto laws), section 17 (right to assemble and petition), section 19 (right to remedy and justice), and section 23 (preliminary hearings). The portion of section 14 relating to the state's immunity to suit was postponed to June 17 and at that time ruled out of order by reason of the adoption of a general government proposal on the same subject. In section 17 the phrase "to associate freely," added in committee, was deleted.

The following day, June 4, only two sections — section 2 (due process of law and equal protection) and section 6 (searches, seizures, interceptions, and privacy) — were approved. As to section 2, the minority report, urging the deletion of the phrase "including the unborn," was approved 80 to 32 after an extensive and exciting debate. Four amendments to section 6 were defeated before first reading approval of the section.

On June 5, section 13 (right of eminent domain) was amended to delete the reference to "impaired use" as the basis for compensation and amended also to delete the requirement for compensation to "full extent of loss"; then the section was approved. The same day the majority preamble was approved after the defeat of the minority report.

On June 9, four sections were considered, some with extended debate. Section 21 (rights retained) was readily approved. Section 22 (freedom from discrimination in employment and property) was approved with relative ease, 90 to 6, despite the prior fears that it might face the difficulties that open housing and fair employment proposals always encountered in the General Assembly. Section 24 (public employees) was deleted after a struggle, when the minority report against any provision on the subject was approved. Section 25 (basic needs) failed to obtain the 59 votes required by the convention rules and was sent back to the committee, which took no further action on it.

The next day, June 10, two sections — section 26 (individual dignity) by a vote of 60 to 27 after acrimonious debate, and section 7 (bail and habeas corpus) by a vote of 82 to 0 — were approved. The approval of section 26 was preceded by the defeat of the minority report which urged that no such section be added to the bill of rights. Unanimous approval of section 7 had been preceded by a debate on the minority report, subsequently defeated, which favored liberalizing bail provisions.

The same day the authors of the unsuccessful report on bail, Gertz, Raby, and Weisberg, prevailed with their minority report on liberalized provisions as to fines in criminal cases, and section 12 (imprisonment for debt) was approved as amended by the minority report.

The next day, June 11, there was a classical debate on section 27 (right to arms). The minority report of Gertz, Raby, and Weisberg, opposing such provision, was defeated, and the majority section 27 approved 86 to 16. The minority made more noise than the vote indicated.

The same day, the suggested sections on consumer protection proposed by David Stahl and individual privacy proposed by Paul Edward were defeated.

Now the preamble and bill of rights were in the hands of the Committee on Style, Drafting and Submission to prepare for second reading.

But after this cursory summary of the preamble and bill of rights on first reading, it would be well to retrace the situation and tell some of the more exciting episodes of the floor debate. Space does not permit a full account of the debate or even any substantial segment of it.

Some of the motivation that went into the strong vote on the right to arms provision was described for me by delegate Ralph Dunn from DuQuoin in southern Illinois. Dunn called himself and Buford, Butler, Hendren, and Kenney the "Mountaineers." Dunn felt, instinctively, regardless of his own beliefs, that the people in this area would not be too enthusiastic about the new rights that we set forth in the bill of rights, save for the gun section. But he knew that our committee was one of the true sights of the convention, and he made it a point to have his visiting constituents spend time with us. He would point out Father Lawlor, Raby, and myself as "a distinguished and famous group" and tell of my activities in the Leopold and Ruby cases and, "if it was a proper audience," of Father Lawlor's fetus. Dunn was not a gun owner nor a hunter, but he knew his people. So when some of his constituents — the Pinckneyville Business and Professional Women's Club — were in the visitors' gallery, he made his famous speech in support of the gun section, knowing that word of it would be taken to the folks back home. He said, in the highly personalized fashion that distinguished him:

> People in Southern Illinois perhaps are closer to frontier days than some of you urban dwellers. Many of our ancestors came from Virginia through Tennessee and Kentucky and settled in Illinois not too many generations ago. If someone tried to take my grand-

father's gun away from him, that person would have suffered bodily harm!

And I'm sure you know, people in our district are very much opposed to the present gun-owners registration law. Representative Gale Williams has won great fame and honor in his district by leading the fight for repeal of this onerous law. Had this proposed amendment never been offered, no one would have felt injured, but since it has been proposed, to not pass it will make the people of Southern Illinois feel that a right has been taken away. I submit the feeling among our people is that gun registration is a first step toward confiscation of weapons.

I submit that guns still serve many useful purposes in Southern Illinois: many a father has a shotgun in his closet that is used on certain social occasions. I certainly don't want to deny him that privilege.

I had assumed that the Cook County Democrats would oppose the provision when the corporation counsel of Chicago, Richard L. Curry, the mayor's own cousin, sent Marvin Aspen, a personal representative, to the Bill of Rights Committee to correct the impression given by Leonard Foster that the proposed gun provision was agreeable to him. Aspen and the chief of detectives of Chicago, Michael Spiotto, made it clear that they favored the most rigid gun control. But Paul Elward, for long an advocate of such control in the General Assembly, declared, with amazing conviction: "For the first time we are getting constitutional underpinning for gun control legislation. This invalidates no existing law or ordinance." He added piously: "We need less violence in our society, verbal as well as physical."

That was the very reason I could not understand why the "Daley cohorts," as I described them in an appeal to the convention, were going along with the gun proponents. I read some comments by Daley in the morning press when gun violence against the police was reported. Guns will be used when they are around, I stressed. Weisberg made an even more eloquent plea in behalf of our minority report, as did some of the best men and women at the convention. But we were fortunate to receive as many as forty votes for our report, considering the unnatural ganging up against us. That was our high tide. Following the defeat of our report, the majority proposal won 86 to 16. That was what almost invariably happened at the convention. Once the opposition was downed, many who had favored its viewpoint would swing to the majority viewpoint. That is why one must study the interim votes in order to size up a situation accurately.

The mayor's own son, Richard Daley, with whom I had enjoyed an excellent personal relationship, reacted strongly to my use of the phrase, "Daley's cohorts." He read into it a critical spirit that was not intended, and I thought it politic to say so in a speech in response in which I stressed my long-time support of Daley, despite our differences. On another occasion I reminded the party stalwarts, such as Elward, that I had been a registered Democrat for forty years. This prompted young Michael Madigan to come up to me in front of the whole body and say, "Elmer, do me a favor — don't register as a Democrat next time." Even the most serious debates were relieved by such by-plays. For myself, I was content to be judged by such staunch Democrats as Thomas McCracken and Philip Carey, rather than the shrill partisans, who made it so difficult to reach a consensus on any issue.

While the first-reading debate was still going on in the convention committee of the whole as to the bill of rights, the *Chicago Sun-Times* published one of its numerous editorials on our work: It said:

> We have found occasion for both criticism and praise, because the Bill of Rights contains sensitive, controversial, even volatile, matter. Still to be debated, for instance, is an unfortunate freeing up of the right to keep and bear arms. Our stand there is well known. We favor more control, not less.
>
> Nonetheless, we think it proper that the committee which constructed the proposed Bill of Rights be credited for a difficult job well done.

The editorial told of the dedicated spirit in which we had worked, on committee and in the general sessions of the convention, and concluded:

> We commend the Bill of Rights Committee, a disparate group of individuals, for doing as well as it has with this basic democratic task.[2]

[2] Editorial, "A document in democracy," *Chicago Sun-Times*, June 7, 1970.

On the day we were to take up the due process clause Father Lawlor offered the invocation, significant in view of the day's business. The grim priest preached on the sacredness of life. "Help us," he implored, "to respect this right to life which You give to all others." He gave, in brief compass and in the guise of a prayer, the arguments against destroying "those in need, the poor, the blind, the lame, the lepers" and, by implication, although he did not directly say so, the human fetus. Some minutes later, we sat as a committee of the whole, and President Witwer called upon me to proceed with the discussion on the work of the Bill of Rights Committee. I aroused laughter by saying: "We don't have dissenting votes on invocations, but it was a very stirring invocation and the start of the debate I take it."

It was now Arthur Lennon's task to defend the use of the words "including the unborn" in the due process and equal protection section. Lennon, a very shrewd and resourceful debater, made the most of the troublesome phrase, largely in terms of the majority report, but spelling out why he contended that the language was not revolutionary or extreme and consistent with what he deemed the law to be. Other delegates quickly interrogated Lennon, starting with the brilliant young man from Evanston, Frank Cicero, one of the group of Independents. The interrogation became a debate, improper at that phase of the proceedings, in which Leonard Foster and I expressed differences as to whether the phrase applied only to due process or as to equal protection as well. I asked Lennon if the phrase "including the unborn" included "the very moment of conception." He hedged, I thought uncomfortably, in his response. I asked if the provision was self-implementing or if it would require legislation. Again, I thought he hedged.

Now one after the other delegate got into the fray; their questions, like mine and Cicero's, being a form of argumentation. It was clear that almost everyone wanted to say something on this highly controversial subject in which the convention was taking sides so noticeably. The women, the blacks, the Independents and Downstaters were sharply opposed to the proposed language; the Daley Democrats strongly for it. Lennon fielded the questions with great skill, but he was persuading only the persuaded. Dwight Friedrich got to the heart of the matter at once. He pointed out that Father Lawlor suggested that life begins with fertilization, and Rabbi Hershman, who one day had given the invocation, said that in the Jewish faith life begins when the baby's head protrudes from the womb. Did this not make it a religious question, and was that not undesirable?

Again, I wanted to inquire as to what facts or circumstances caused Lennon as an individual to sponsor the inclusion of the phrase. He thought I was arguing with him and he would not answer the question. Helen Kinney wanted to know the effect of the phrase on laws relating to abortion. Lennon would not give an unequivocal response.

The questions concluded for the moment, Lewis Wilson presented the minority views, I thought quite persuasively. He did not hedge. He was blunt in stating his belief that the supporters of the majority report were intent upon preventing legislation to permit abortions. His argument for the minority report was supplemented by Bernard Weisberg, as always shrewd in his analysis of constitutional, legislative, and practical issues. It was easy to understand why his coldly rational tone disconcerted those as emotionally involved as Kelleghan.

Now Father Lawlor interposed what he regarded as questions and what President Witwer believed to be argumentation, scheduled to come at a later stage. Father Lawlor stressed his interest in life — when did it arise, when and how was it to be protected. Now Wilson, now Weisberg, answered questions, as Father Lawlor persisted in his line of quasi-interrogation. Others joined in, some with much heat.

The questions on the minority report concluded, I moved the substitution of the minority report, which excluded the words "including the unborn," for the majority report which included those controversial words. One delegate was applauded when he inquired why we could not proceed to a vote at once, since everyone had obviously made up his mind on the subject. President Witwer properly insisted that the only way to test the matter was to ask who wanted to discuss the matter, as permitted by the rules.

With great emotion Clyde Parker, who was opposed to capital punishment, declared that by reason of the same respect for life, he was for the majority report, which he said was on the side of life.

Father Lawlor quickly joined in. He complained about the effort to stifle debate; then went on and on in his deeply felt defense of life against those who would trifle with it. As he had exceeded the ten minutes allowed by the rules, President Witwer interrupted him. "The system must go on," the Father commented. "Thank you." Witwer stung, assured him that he would have further opportunity for debate.

When the debate resumed after the luncheon recess, Leonard Foster proclaimed that he agreed completely with the statements made by Father Lawlor, but disagreed completely with his conclusion. Kelleghan inveighed against those like Paul Ehrlich who would equate life with pollution. Life to him was sacred, and he would protect it by safeguarding the due process rights of the unborn. Rev. Joseph Sharpe, a black delegate, strongly seconded Kelleghan in the name of God. He was answered by Albert Raby. Once again the convention had the opportunity to observe the moderation and reasonableness of Raby in contrast to his reputation in some corners as an extremist.

Paul Mathias wanted to move the previous question, so that debate would be terminated. President Witwer feared that this would indicate an unwillingness to hear out arguments on both sides. He did not put the question. Young Peter Tomei, a devout Catholic, rose to state his conviction that matters of conscience should not be ruled out in the manner of the majority report. He was for the minority position. So the debate went on, some almost trembling with emotion, others having at least the outer aspect of calm and reasonableness. Father Lawlor took the floor once more in his defense of life against those who would destroy it. Clifford Kelley rose to question Father Lawlor's right to speak again; but the president, following the advice of the parliamentarian, said that Lawlor was in order, and he went on, eloquently, obviously unable to see how there could be differences of opinion on the subject.

Betty Howard, a tall, lovely and articulate delegate from the suburbs, did oppose him "as a woman, a wife, a mother, and a Christian." Henry Hendren pleaded that the matter go to a vote. President Witwer asked Lennon to sum up for the majority and he did so in a manner that seemed to create differences in viewpoint between himself and Lawlor, whether of strategy or conviction one could not be sure.

Then debate on this important subject was interrupted while Harold Nudelman complained of the camera lights of the media and President Witwer attempted to explain why freedom of the press could not be interfered with. Nudelman was unsatisfied. John Knuppel tried to talk without being recognized by the chair, and his microphone was cut off. Thus did tempers rise with the tenseness of the discussion.

Finally, Lewis Wilson was permitted to conclude for the minority, and the voting began, with Victor Arrigo and others explaining their votes, as permitted by the rules. Seldom did more delegates feel like explaining themselves, both for the record and their consciences.

The motion to substitute the minority report for the committee majority was carried by 80 to 32. Despite all the debate, it was not even close. The motion to approve the minority report, as substituted, a technical necessity, was then carried 92 to 8. The convention had overcome what might have been one of the greatest obstacles towards the approval of any new constitution.

There is much that can be said about the effort to abolish the death penalty, and, for clarity, it should be said in one place, rather than broken up in segments. I have always had great moral fervor against the ancient and barbaric institution of capital punishment. I have filed *amici curiae* briefs in death cases in the United States Supreme Court in behalf of the American Civil Liberties Union, various religious denominations, and others, and have made countless speeches and written many articles on the subject. Naturally, I filed a member proposal on abolition when I became a delegate, but I gave hard thought to the advisability of impairing the chances of the approval of the proposed constitution by pushing abolition. I talked over the matter with Bernard Weisberg, who felt as strongly as I did and whose judgment I respected. Despite the strong and moving testimony that was introduced, we decided against going through with a committee vote on the matter.

Then the section on penalties after conviction came up before the convention. Wayne Whalen, seconded by Robert Canfield, a former state's attorney, and Philip Carey, a Daley Democrat, moved an amendment to ban the death penalty. Now that the issue was raised, I felt under the moral compulsion to support the amendment and I did as much as anyone in its behalf. Much to my amazement, we lost by a narrow vote, 54 to 50, despite the strong opposition of Paul Elward and other retributive-minded delegates. As I left the chamber following the vote, a number of delegates, including Lewis Wilson, volunteered that if there were a separate submission on abolition, they would support it. For the first time, I developed a degree of optimism and began to work diligently toward adoption of a separate submission proposal. Although it remained the Whalen-Canfield-Carey proposal, I think that my role was at least as important in lining up support. Clifford Kelley, a young black delegate, was of the greatest help to us. Almost all of the blacks were with us, including Democratic organization stalwarts like Odas Nicholson. On second reading we prevailed. By third reading, I personally was able to win over some of the opponents, and we won handily. This was fortunate, as some of the supporters were not around when the vote was taken. Thus are issues decided in any deliberative body! For the first time, I permitted myself a large degree of optimism.

Then came the time when we were supposed to line up popular support for the separate submission on abolition. The Illinois Committee for the Abolition of Capital Punishment mounted a campaign for the proposal, with the renowned lawyer, Albert Jenner, Jr., as honorary chairman, and Hans Mattick, Willard Lassers, and me as the active leaders. We had a budget and a staff and probably the best literature of any written on the separately submitted proposals. We used the radio and television, the churches, and the black community. There was no active campaign against the proposition. Neither political party took a stand. For years public opinion polls had shown an increasing percentage of the people against the death penalty — until the law-and-order syndrome set in. I debated with the state's attorney of Cook County over television and seemed to win on points. But when the votes were counted, abolition suffered a worse defeat than any other proposition. It was a disaster. The reasons? Perhaps, because I was the only delegate to devote considerable effort to the campaign; a few others did a bit, but only a bit. Wayne Whalen, quite properly, was too busy on the judicial selection proposition. It may have been the Speck case, the times. At any rate, we lost badly.

One of those who participated most effectively in the debate on the section relating to preliminary hearings was John M. Karns, Jr., chairman of the committee on finance and revenue who, when state's attorney of his county, had employed William Fennoy as an investigator. Karns and Fennoy did not look at the preliminary hearing proposal in the same light. Feeling it important to incorporate the views of Karns on this important matter, I elicited this comment from him, which brought forth some of the "secret history" of the convention:

> As you will recall, I testified before your committee and was also active in debate before the convention on the inclusion of a provision requiring a preliminary hearing as a matter of constitutional right.
>
> My thoughts on this can be summed up briefly: to my knowledge, no other state constitution nor the Constitution of the United States (see *Coleman* v. *State of Alabama*)[3] requires a preliminary hearing as a matter of constitutional right; additionally, I felt the matter was adequately covered in the Illinois Code of Criminal Procedure.
>
> I understand that the committee did include such a provision in its report on first reading, largely at the insistence of my fellow delegate, William Fennoy, who in my opinion, had some mistaken notions about the efficacy of a preliminary hearing as an important protection of the rights of accused.
>
> On first reading, I moved the deletion of the provision which I recall then carried. In argument supporting my motion, I advanced the idea that certain investigations are only effective if brought initially before a grand jury, particularly those dealing with crimes of public officials and certain types of organized criminal activities such as gambling, and to require preliminary hearings in such instances would legally destroy the grand jury as an effective investigative tool in those types of investigations.
>
> After the provision was initially deleted, Delegate Parkhurst moved

[3] 391 U.S. 1, 26 L. Ed. 2d 387, 90 S. Ct. 387.

a substitute provision that presently appears as Paragraph 2, Section 7 of the Bill of Rights. I was curious at that time about John's interest in these matters and was later informed that he did this at the request of President Witwer who, for some reason, was interested in some provision regarding preliminary hearings appearing in the Bill of Rights.

I might add, the matter was further complicated by the decision of the Supreme Court in the *Coleman* case, which held that a preliminary hearing is a critical stage of the prosecution and may require the appointment of counsel to an indigent defendant in some circumstances. It should be noted, however, that *Coleman* does not hold that a preliminary hearing is a constitutionally mandated requirement.

I might add, that I don't particularly have a strong feeling in the matter since I feel that the provision as written adds nothing to the requirements already contained in the Illinois Code of Criminal Procedure. I would assume that this is a right which the defendant may waive, and in my experience, usually would waive.

David Stahl, Mayor Daley's administrative assistant, was one of the most hard-working and effective delegates. At times he strayed from his organization colleagues on his votes and in the proposals he put forth. Feeling that a personal note might lend intimacy to this narrative, I wrote to Stahl for his comments. He replied:

As your parenthetical note indicates, my activities with respect to your Committee centered principally around the consumer rights issue, although I did introduce several proposals regarding the arts which, as I recall, were referred to your committee.

I suspect that the transcript of the Convention and the roll call on first reading says all that really needs to be said about the consumer rights effort. As you will recall, my proposal was first referred to the Rules Committee where it almost died. With the intervention of several friends on the Rules Committee it was referred to the Legislative Committee rather than dying in Rules. With the consent of George Lewis and yourself, it was informally reassigned to the Bill of Rights Committee but because of the excitement which your Committee was constantly creating, it never got a hearing before your Committee. The transcript should reflect President Witwer's impatience with my amendment as well as the concern he expressed to me that the whole debate and consideration of the matter not take more than an hour. As I recollect, we spent an hour and fifteen minutes on the floor discussing consumer rights although many of those who spoke for the amendment did much more by way of presentation of their remarks.

While I don't regard the loss of the consumer rights section as a great calamity, it would have been another reason for people to vote for the new Constitution. With regard to specifically what we proposed, I must admit we had a terrible time getting the right language and I suspect it was defeated because we didn't ever get the right solution to the semantics problem of saying what we really meant.

Stahl expressed a dilemma that beset others. If he who was so articulate — he was chairman of the convention's Public Information Committee — had such difficulty, imagine the difficulty of others.

The delegates were an introspective group, often analyzing themselves and others as if they were characters in a Russian novel. Still, they were Americans, with great faith in gadgets and computers in particular, and thought that statistical tables, questionnaires, polls, and mere numbers had great meaning. They, especially the members of the Bill of Rights Committee, were all intrigued when rumbles arose as to an ideological rating of delegates by the young vice-president of the convention, John Alexander, somewhat of a political pundit. He took seven pivotal issues that were voted on in the course of the first reading of the bill of rights and for each favorable vote on each of them he gave one point. The perfect liberal would have seven points; the fewer points you had, the less liberal you were. It was simplicity itself. Charles N. Wheeler III told the whole story in an exclusive feature article in the *Chicago Sun-Times*.[4]

Paul Elward called it "a silly waste of time and not an accurate reflection of anybody's political philosophy," but he had voted liberal, according to Alexander's test, only once. Convention Vice-President Thomas G. Lyons, who also had voted liberal only once,

[4] Charles N. Wheeler III, "Ideological rating a surprise to many at Con-Con," *Chicago Sun-Times,* June 21, 1970.

commented: "I don't think my liberal record is going to be tarnished by this survey." Thomas Kelleghan rated o by the Alexander test. On the other hand, young Jeffrey R. Ladd, who considered himself a "conservative, responsible Republican," was disturbed that he was found to be in the upper levels of liberalism with a 6. "The study is very unscientific," he said. Did this lead him ultimately to cast the one vote against the bill of rights on final reading? The human psyche is sometimes peculiar, to say the least. I, who rated a 7, naturally thought Alexander's study "basically sound." I observed smugly: "It's the most interesting document to come out of the convention so far."

According to Alexander, you were a liberal if you voted *for* (1) the elimination of the alleged federally unconstitutional clause in the freedom of speech section; (2) abolition of capital punishment; and (3) extending the right of collective bargaining to public employees; and if you voted *against* (1) deletion of the provision requiring a prompt preliminary hearing for persons charged with felonies; (2) including the unborn in the due process section; (3) an amendment to the antidiscrimination section intended to protect property owner's rights; and (4) the right to bear arms section.

The majority of the convention had favored the liberal position on three of the issues and had voted against on four of the issues. Ultimately, it had restored the balance somewhat by voting for separate submission on one of the issues.

The members of the Bill of Rights Committee rated as follows:

Chicago members		*Suburban members*	
Victor A. Arrigo	2	John E. Dvorak	5
Leonard N. Foster	4	Thomas C. Kelleghan	o
Elmer Gertz	7	Arthur T. Lennon	2
James Kemp	5	Virginia B. Macdonald	4
Father Francis S. Lawlor	2	Roy C. Pechous	3
Albert A. Raby	7	*Downstate members*	
Bernard Weisberg	7	William F. Fennoy, Jr.	2
		(plus two absences)	
		Matthew A. Hutmacher	1
		Lewis D. Wilson	5

Thus, as might have been expected, Gertz, Raby, and Weisberg, who so often joined in minority reports, were at the top as liberals, with 7 points each; Kelleghan was the least liberal, with no points, closely followed by Hutmacher with one point, Arrigo, Father Lawlor, and Lennon each with two points (omitting Fennoy because of absences); in the center were Kemp, Dvorak, and Wilson, each with 5 points. One could play with these figures, as Alexander did, and come up with such interesting facts as that the Republicans and Democrats as a whole were 3.1 in rating, just below the middle; Independents as a whole were near the top with 6.3; suburban delegates were somewhat more liberal than Chicago delegates, 4 to 3.3, while Downstaters were 3.1; the women averaged 5.3, while the men averaged 3.1; over-all the convention delegates rated about neutral — 3.4.

What this meant at the time, or would mean as the convention progressed, was not readily foreseeable. Other ratings were made, the most scientific by David Connor, the banker delegate from Peoria. He had his computers show how each delegate compared in voting with every other delegate on first, second, and third readings. The ratios differed somewhat from reading to reading, but they told a significant story. There was no effort by the computer, or by Connor, to describe anyone as liberal, conservative, radical, or reactionary; but there was raw material for all sorts of analogies. At one point, for example, Albert Raby and President Witwer had the greatest degree of similarity in voting patterns; on one reading I was closest to Weisberg, on another to Dawn Clark Netsch and Frank Cicero. The latter, Italian in origin like Arrigo, had petulantly passed his vote on the bill of rights on one occasion, as I recall, because of his disgust over Arrigo's individual dignity provision.

I have already stressed my great confidence in Lewis Wilson, despite our very considerable differences in political philosophy. In writing to me after the convention was over and the constitution adopted, he pointed out certain things about our committee that I may not have stressed sufficiently:

> I believe the striking characteristic of our Committee was the diversity in background and experience of its fifteen members. I doubt that this was equalled by any other Committee.
>
> We had Republicans, regular Democrats, Independent Democrats; Jews, Catholics and Protestants; blacks and whites; one woman;

ultra-conservatives (I believe I am in this category) and liberals; strong "party" people (e.g., Arrigo, Lennon, Macdonald) and those who were not; at least one strong labor man (Kemp) and at least one who had always been allied into the management side (myself).

Only geographically was such complete diversity lacking. There were 7 members from Chicago itself and 5 more from the Chicago metropolis area — a total of 12 of the fifteen. That left three of us from downstate. All of us were from cities along the Mississippi and at least two of us (Fennoy and I) were from industrial areas — and the same is true of Hutmacher to a somewhat less extent. Outside of Fennoy, possibly, there was no member of the Committee from that great portion (geographically) of the State from Springfield south to the Ohio river.

I assume the answer to this is that most of the Bill of Rights problems arise in the Chicago area, for obvious reasons, and therefore, this area should have predominant representation. I am not sure, however, that this is a wholly good answer.

I think it is in order to note that two of the Committee members opposed the Constitution as finally adopted (Kelleghan and Kemp). . . . In view of the fact that only a very few of the total number of delegates opposed the Constitution, I would feel our Committee had a higher percentage of its members in opposition than did any other Committee.

On July 2, 1970, the bill of rights article came out of the Committee on Style, Drafting and Submission very little changed, but lacking for the time being the preamble, still being considered by that committee. In the last weeks of the convention, this committee, chaired by the brilliant and resourceful young battler from Hanover, Wayne W. Whalen, was probably the busiest and most successful of all the committees of the convention. Whalen, elected as a Democrat, was part of the Independent bloc which included Gertz, Raby, and Weisberg of the Bill of Rights Committee. These Independents and their associates and sometime allies frequently conferred and often coordinated their efforts. Each was a distinct personality, conscientious and independent in a thoroughgoing sense. Yet, on basic matters, they generally followed a similar voting pattern, however their reasoning and manner differed.

Lewis Wilson was vice-chairman of Whalen's committee and, in a sense, the representative of the Bill of Rights Committee on Style and Drafting. The chairman and counsel of Style and Drafting conferred with me on all proposed changes in the bill of rights and, to make certain that there would be no uproar, we also conferred with other members of the committee. We were trying to make certain that some sort of consensus would be achieved.

Style and Drafting suggested that the old section on subordination of military power be moved to the militia article and that the section on elections be moved, as suggested by Peter Tomei, to the article on suffrage and elections. Nobody objected and the removals were accomplished as a matter of course. Whether or not the changes in location had any effect constitutionally remains to be seen, but it is extremely doubtful.

Style and Drafting also contemplated the removal of Dwight Friedrich's language about individual obligations and responsibilities to the preamble, but in the end it remained in the section on fundamental principles, where it had initially been placed and where it really belonged.

The section on preliminary hearing in criminal matters was added to the section on indictment as suggested by the Bill of Rights Committee. It was obviously a good decision.

For the rest, the proposed changes were truly stylistic, as contemplated when the role of the Style and Drafting Committee was delineated. Punctuation was added, subtracted or changed; words of greater clarity were substituted for those of lesser clarity; in all, the language was tightened up, so that the meaning of each section became self-evident. Where the exigencies of convention realities required it, the sometimes archaic language of the older sections, redolent with tradition, was retained.

One change in the order of language in the amended section on searches, seizures, privacy, and interceptions strengthened the section substantively, I thought. By placing the phrase "invasions of privacy" after "seizures," instead of at the end of the sequence, the committee had given the phrase body and blood. It was no longer a dangling and perhaps useless limb.

Following the completion of second reading in plenary session, the report of the Style, Drafting and Submission Committee en-

compassed the entire new constitution, including proposed separate submissions, committee recommendations, and the transition
schedule. Very little in the way of textual changes was proposed for
the preamble and the bill of rights. There was again new language
to clarify the meaning of preliminary hearings in criminal cases.
The new concept of the goal of rehabilitation in penalties was
phrased more precisely. A new section prohibiting discrimination on
the basis of sex, proposed and approved on the floor of the convention, was rephrased to conform with the requirements of other
articles. Otherwise the language changes were minor.

In conformity with the floor vote on second reading, there were
two separate submissions with respect to the bill of rights — whether
to add the sentence, "No penalty shall prescribe death," in section
11 on limitation of penalties after conviction, and whether to add
a new section with respect to nondiscrimination for the physically or
mentally handicapped. It was already apparent that the latter proposed separate submission, forced by some who should have favored
the inclusion of the section in the body of the constitution, was creating troubled spirits and rebellion. At third reading there was
heated discussion of the matter which was resolved by inclusion of
the provision in the bill of rights.

Third reading was the final stage in the proceedings; substantial
amendments and substitutions were no longer freely permitted. For
such changes the rules required, in the first instance, suspension of
the rules by a constitutional majority, amounting to fifty-nine, and
then passage by at least the same vote. When Style, Drafting and
Submission presented its report, under date of August 26, 1970,
with very little time left for us to complete our work, it was doubtful
that the convention would tolerate many suspensions of the rules.
But surprise is the overriding rule of conventions, as well as of life,
and one could look forward to fireworks, whether confidently or
tensely.

The transition schedule declared that any rights, procedural or
substantive, created for the first time by the bill of rights article,
would be prospective and not retroactive. There could be no objection to this; and it was probably implicit anyway in due process.
Section 17, relating to nondiscrimination in employment and property, was to become effective on July 1, 1971, reasonable in view

of the newness and far-reaching consequences of the rights created.

On August 27, 1970, Wayne Whalen, as chairman of the Style, Drafting and Submission Committee, presented for third reading the proposed new constitution with the changes made by his committee following approval on second reading. Point by point he first took up the preamble and the bill of rights, indicating exactly what had been done by his committee and why. Question was raised by the always attentive Thomas McCracken as to whether or not a substantive change was inadvertently made in the section on discrimination with respect to sex. Delegates Cicero, Leahy, Parkhurst, and Kamin rose to the defense of the committee. It appeared probable that the convention was going to be bogged down again on some relatively unimportant detail at the very time when it was necessary to proceed with greater speed than ever before. At that point, I suggested that we vote on the rest of the preamble and bill of rights and reserve judgment on the section that had aroused the controversy. This was approved by the convention and at last, as far as language was concerned, approval was voted.

The next day, August 28, on further consideration, I withdrew my earlier request for the separate submission of the section prohibiting discrimination on the basis of sex and moved that the preamble and bill of rights be approved at third and final reading and for preparation for enrollment. Yet, again, there were impediments to speedy action. David Connor had been interrogated by the chief of police in Peoria as to the section which incorporated the ban on unreasonable invasions of privacy and interceptions of communications. He wanted to know what invasion of privacy meant, how it would affect visual surveillance by the police, how it would affect the performance of other ordinary duties by those charged with law enforcement. The chief of police had thought that the provision might impair the efficiency of law enforcement agencies. I tried to explain as best I could why I felt that the fears were unreasonable. I was referred to a case pending in the United States Supreme Court and since then decided adversely to the contention of those who wanted a complete ban on all electronic surveillance and interceptions. I pointed out that Bernard Weisberg and other members of our committee felt that single-party consent would still govern and thus the police might in certain designated circumstances intercept communications. Foster was not sure that my explanation was correct. I did not agree with much of what he said, but I felt it inadvisable to spell out my differences and simply pointed out that we would all have to wait for court interpretation of the provision.

Past that hurdle, Father Lawlor now confronted us with another hurdle. He wanted us to combine the sections on nondiscrimination against the handicapped and on the basis of sex. Regretfully, I raised a point of order — the necessity for suspension of the rules — and was sustained by President Witwer. Suspension of the rules was moved, but the motion failed. Section 19 relating to nondiscrimination with respect to the physically and mentally handicapped had been added to the bill of rights the previous day. It was no longer a matter of separate submission.

The clerk proceeded with the roll call of delegates on the motion for the final passage of the bill of rights and preamble and all went on swimmingly until Odas Nicholson was reached. She was troubled because I had withdrawn my motion for a division which separated section 18 (nondiscrimination on the basis of sex) from the total package. Miss Nicholson disagreed with me that there was no longer need for a division. By a narrow vote the roll call was suspended and she was given leave to make whatever point she chose to make. Miss Nicholson said she wanted to have the changes made by the Style, Drafting and Submission Committee replaced by the language that had appeared in the section when it was adopted on second reading. The latter, she believed, was more inclusive. Wayne Whalen explained again why he thought this was wrong. Miss Nicholson was not persuaded. There followed an exchange between the two which was not always clear to the other delegates. I tried to resolve the matter again by pointing out that in any case equal protection of the laws would protect women in this area completely. Foster agreed that there was nothing in section 18 that was not already covered by the due process and equal protection of the laws section. Miss Nicholson made cutting remarks with respect to Foster's pronouncement. We seemed to be stalled once again. I moved that we proceed with the roll call and, to my relief, there was no objection. Gloria Pughsley remarked that she had to pass, when roll call was resumed, because she did not want the matter to be railroaded through without satisfying Miss Nicholson's question. Finally, the preamble and bill of rights were approved with only one nay vote but with fourteen passing. Those of us on the Bill of Rights Committee had thus accomplished our objective more readily than we had dared hope when the convention began months previously.

More than a year after the adjournment of the convention, Jeffrey Ladd, who had cast the one negative vote, told me the reasons for his opposition, since then somewhat softened. First and foremost, he was enraged by what he regarded as the cowardice of the assembly in voting for Arrigo's section on individual dignity and for the right to arms provision, known by both sides, he felt, to be meaningless if not mischievous. He was afraid of the self-implementing aspect of the section on nondiscrimination, and he thought the women's rights section and the provision on the handicapped were hypocritical. Ladd is a practical, unsentimental, and earnest young man who does not believe in pretense or the rhetorical. When he discussed his viewpoint with me, I made no effort to influence his judgment although I strongly disagreed with him.

As the three readings went on in the convention, with the ensuing excitement of debate and votes and public discussion on the reports of the various committees, it became increasingly clear that the early impression of our committee was changing. Where once there was hostility, amusement, bewilderment, and the feeling of impending disaster, there was now friendliness, admiration, and a sense of triumph. This was reflected in the media and even more in the conversation of delegates. Constantly, men and women would come up to me to express their regard for what we had done and how we had handled ourselves in the convention. It was not alone those in our own camp who were almost buoyant in what they had to say. That archconservative, Ted Borek, talked almost in wonderment as to how the Bill of Rights Committee had prevailed where others had failed. It was not that Borek was in agreement with us; quite to the contrary. But he admired a workmanlike job. Thomas McCracken, most respected of the organization Democrats, on more than one occasion said to me, "Elmer, I admire you, even when I disagree. You know what you want, and you are not diverted."

And Victor Arrigo, in that deep, resonant voice of his, would constantly coo over how we had handled ourselves. "We are models for the convention," he intoned.

This was not wholly fortuitous. I had made up my mind before our report was presented to the convention that I would studiously avoid affronting those upon whom we depended for votes. Despite my strong feelings on many issues, I determinedly restricted my participation in the debates — until our report was under consideration. Then I utilized all of the built up goodwill. I tried to field the discussion. On the microphone and away from it, I put forth the most persuasive arguments I could muster. But I did not monopolize the time of the convention or, indeed, of the committee. I pushed forward everyone who could help, whether it was Foster, Lennon, Weisberg, Wilson, or anyone else. So a new reputation was created, and we all basked in it.

A number of sections were born on the floor of the convention or outside of Springfield, rather than in committee. An intriguing example of this is the provision which is now section 5 (pension and retirement rights) in the general provisions article of the constitution. Late in the life of our committee I began to receive an extraordinary number of communications on the pension and retirement rights of government employees, particularly those connected with state universities. These people were sold the idea that their rights were imperiled and that they would be left destitute or, at the very least prejudiced, unless the bill of rights contained a protective provision in their behalf. I received hundreds, if not thousands, of letters and petitions from them. No delegate received more communications on any one theme than I received on this one. I was almost overwhelmed, and troubled. It became a subject of conversation among delegates and the staff. I had the matter researched by a bright young staff assistant, and wrote to all of the many who had written to me. Frankly, I was not sure as to what could properly be done in the constitution, assuming, as was not certain, that there was really a problem. Suddenly delegate Helen Kinney came up with a proposal on the matter, listing several sponsors but not myself! After insistence on my part, my name was added to the list, and the proposal was approved by the convention. There was much pride of authorship at the convention. Success or failure would often depend upon whose name was signed to a proposal; likewise approval or disapproval back home.

Chapters could be written about each battle as to each provision on the convention floor, during each of the three readings, and in the secret conclaves and caucuses where delegates foregathered. The temptation is great to spin out the fascinating tale in its manifold details, telling about the heroes and villains and fainthearted in each struggle. Some decisions were close, some overwhelming, some unexpected, some according to plan.

Two sections proposed by the Bill of Rights Committee — on basic needs and the rights of public employees — were eliminated completely on first reading; basic needs because a constitutional majority was not obtained, the rights of public employees because the Cook County Democrats joined with certain Downstaters against it. Two ancient sections, on free and equal elections and subordination of military power, were transferred to other articles by the Style and Drafting Committee; and two new sections — no discrimination on the basis of sex and no discrimination against the handicapped — were added, the first with virtually no struggle and the second after considerable maneuvering and pressure. As to some sections there were very considerable debates, but in the end the sections were left largely as we had recommended them; other sections were expanded or contracted and considerably modified on the floor.

It proved to be easier than anticipated to get rid of the mischievous phrase "including the unborn" in the due process clause; the women and the blacks, the Independents, most Republicans and most downstate Democrats united against it, while the bulk of the Cook County Democrats and very few others joined in the futile fight for the phrase.

Despite the support of the Catholic bishops for the retention intact and unchanged of the religious freedom section, there was a group, largely Catholic in composition, that persistently sought to amend the section, as well as the section in the education article against the use of public funds for sectarian purposes, by substituting the general language of the First Amendment of the federal constitution or some other language. Some professed to be constitutional purists; others were frankly in favor of giving assistance to parochial schools.

The bishops thought that this could be done through the present
language; some delegates wanted to make this doubly certain. None
of them reckoned sufficiently with the United States Supreme Court.

There was much less of a struggle than anticipated on the section
against discrimination in employment and the sale or rental of
property. In the end there were no more votes against the provision
in the convention than in committee — a mere half-dozen. This can
be described as one of the miracles of our nine months.

Our section on eminent domain was somewhat mangled, largely
because of those like Charles Young and James Strunck who were
extremely sensitive to the problems of public agencies, having long
represented the government in condemnation matters.

In the end we came up with this preamble and this bill of rights:

PREAMBLE

We, the People of the State of Illinois — grateful to Almighty God
for the civil, political and religious liberty which He has permitted
us to enjoy and seeking His blessing upon our endeavors — in order
to provide for the health, safety and welfare of the people; maintain a representative and orderly government; eliminate poverty and
inequality; assure legal, social and economic justice; provide opportunity for the fullest development of the individual; insure do-
mestic tranquility; provide for the common defense; and secure
the blessings of freedom and liberty to ourselves and our posterity
— do ordain and establish this Constitution for the State of Illinois.

ARTICLE I. BILL OF RIGHTS

Section 1. Inherent and Inalienable Rights

All men are by nature free and independent and have certain inherent and inalienable rights among which are life, liberty and the
pursuit of happiness. To secure these rights and the protection of
property, governments are instituted among men, deriving their just
powers from the consent of the governed.

Section 2. Due Process and Equal Protection

No person shall be deprived of life, liberty or property without due
process of law nor be denied the equal protection of the laws.

Section 3. Religious Freedom

The free exercise and enjoyment of religious profession and worship, without discrimination, shall forever be guaranteed, and no person shall be denied any civil or political right, privilege or capacity, on account of his religious opinions; but the liberty of conscience hereby secured shall not be construed to dispense with oaths or affirmations, excuse acts of licentiousness, or justify practices inconsistent with the peace or safety of the State. No person shall be required to attend or support any ministry or place of worship against his consent, nor shall any preference by[5] given by law to any religious denomination or mode of worship.

Section 4. Freedom of Speech

All persons may speak, write and publish freely, being responsible for the abuse of that liberty. In trials for libel, both civil and criminal, the truth, when published with good motives and for justifiable ends, shall be a sufficient defense.

Section 5. Right to Assemble and Petition

The people have the right to assemble in a peaceable manner, to consult for the common good, to make known their opinions to their representatives and to apply for redress of grievances.

Section 6. Searches, Seizures, Privacy and Interceptions

The people shall have the right to be secure in their persons, houses, papers and other possessions against unreasonable searches, seizures, invasions of privacy or interceptions of communications by eavesdropping devices or other means. No warrant shall issue without probable cause, supported by affidavit particularly describing the place to be searched and the persons or things to be seized.

Section 7. Indictment and Preliminary Hearing

No person shall be held to answer for a criminal offense unless on indictment of a grand jury, except in cases in which the punishment is by fine or by imprisonment other than in the penitentiary, in cases of impeachment, and in cases arising in the militia when in actual service in time of war or public danger. The General Assembly by law may abolish the grand jury or further limit its use.

---

[5] Probably should read "be."

No person shall be held to answer for a crime punishable by death or by imprisonment in the penitentiary unless either the initial charge has been brought by indictment of a grand jury or the person has been given a prompt preliminary hearing to establish probable cause.

Section 8. Rights after Indictment

In criminal prosecutions, the accused shall have the right to appear and defend in person and by counsel; to demand the nature and cause of the accusation and have a copy thereof; to meet the witnesses face to face and to have process to compel the attendance of witnesses in his behalf; and to have a speedy public trial by an impartial jury of the county in which the offense is alleged to have been committed.

Section 9. Bail and Habeas Corpus

All persons shall be bailable by sufficient sureties, except for capital offenses where the proof is evident or the presumption great. The privilege of the writ of habeas corpus shall not be suspended except in cases of rebellion or invasion when the public safety may require it.

Section 10. Self-Incrimination and Double Jeopardy

No person shall be compelled in a criminal case to give evidence against himself nor be twice put in jeopardy for the same offense.

Section 11. Limitation of Penalties after Conviction

All penalties shall be determined both according to the seriousness of the offense and with the objective of restoring the offender to useful citizenship. No conviction shall work corruption of blood or forfeiture of estate. No person shall be transported out of the State for an offense committed within the State.

Section 12. Right to Remedy and Justice

Every person shall find a certain remedy in the laws for all injuries and wrongs which he receives to his person, privacy, property or reputation. He shall obtain justice by law, freely, completely, and promptly.

Section 13. Trial by Jury

The right of trial by jury as heretofore enjoyed shall remain inviolate.

Section 14. *Imprisonment for Debt*

No person shall be imprisoned for debt unless he refuses to deliver up his estate for the benefit of his creditors as provided by law or unless there is a strong presumption of fraud. No person shall be imprisoned for failure to pay a fine in a criminal case unless he has been afforded adequate time to make payment, in installments if necessary, and has willfully failed to make payment.

Section 15. *Right of Eminent Domain*

Private property shall not be taken or damaged for public use without just compensation as provided by law. Such compensation shall be determined by a jury as provided by law.

Section 16. *Ex Post Facto Laws and Impairing Contracts*

No ex post facto law, or law impairing the obligation of contracts or making an irrevocable grant of special privileges or immunities, shall be passed.

Section 17. *No Discrimination in Employment and the Sale or Rental of Property*

All persons shall have the right to be free from discrimination on the basis of race, color, creed, national ancestry and sex in the hiring and promotion practices of any employer or in the sale or rental of property.

These rights are enforceable without action by the General Assembly, but the General Assembly by law may establish reasonable exemptions relating to these rights and provide additional remedies for their violation.

Section 18. *No Discrimination on the Basis of Sex*

The equal protection of the laws shall not be denied or abridged on account of sex by the State or its units of local government and school districts.

Section 19. *No Discrimination Against the Handicapped*

All persons with a physical or mental handicap shall be free from discrimination in the sale or rental of property and shall be free from discrimination unrelated to ability in the hiring and promotion practices of any employer.

Section 20. Individual Dignity

To promote individual dignity, communications that portray criminality, depravity or lack of virtue in, or that incite violence, hatred, abuse or hostility toward, a person or group of persons by reason of or by reference to religious, racial, ethnic, national or regional affiliation are condemned.

Section 21. Quartering of Soldiers

No soldier in time of peace shall be quartered in a house without the consent of the owner; nor in time of war except as provided by law.

Section 22. Right to Arms

Subject only to the police power, the right of the individual citizen to keep and bear arms shall not be infringed.

Section 23. Fundamental Principles

A frequent recurrence to the fundamental principles of civil government is necessary to preserve the blessings of liberty. These blessings cannot endure unless the people recognize their corresponding individual obligations and responsibilities.

Section 24. Rights Retained

The enumeration in this Constitution of certain rights shall not be construed to deny or disparage others retained by the individual citizens of the State.

VII

Reactions and Rejoicings

The last day of the convention was truly memorable. There was little to disturb the grandeur of the occasion, swelled by Mahalia Jackson's singing of the national anthem, President Witwer's measured summing up of our work, the signing of the new charter by each individual delegate at Abraham Lincoln's desk while families beamed with pride. Vice-president Elbert Smith, everyman's favorite humorist, announced that the Bill of Rights Committee had wished its chairman a speedy recovery from an illness by a vote of 8 to 7. The story was apocryphal, but it could have been true. Later in the day, at a party given by the convention staff, I was presented with the Colonel Robert R. McCormick Memorial Award for thirty years of hostility to the *Chicago Tribune,* and my wife, who had daily tended to the needs of delegates, was given the Jewish mother-of-the-year award. Our committee Cassandra, Kelleghan, refused to sign the draft of the new constitution and our vice-chairman, Kemp, signed "in dissent." But Arrigo, ever the good Roman, said by way of farewell: "There is an old Italian saying, 'Every time you say good-bye, you die a little.' That's how most of us feel tonight." There was much more that happened that glorious day. I knew that we would prevail at the polls, despite the doom-sayers. Arrigo just could not let his proposal for individual dignity, for which he had fought and bled so nobly, go down in defeat.

As soon as the general election of November 1970 was out of the way, the *Chicago Tribune* began its advocate's account of the proposed constitution, commencing with extended front and second page coverage of the preamble and bill of rights. Considering the sometimes unsympathetic accounts of the committee and its chairman published in the *Tribune,* this account might almost be called sympathetic. My picture, this time not unflattering, accompanied the article, and I was quoted at length after being described as a "controversial advocate of civil rights" and then as "a longtime American Civil Liberties Union attorney and defender of unpopular causes and personalities."

Each provision was discussed in some detail and rather fairly. John Elmer, one of the two *Tribune* correspondents at the convention, said that the compromises on the right to arms "will help sell the Convention product outside Chicago," and that it also "avoided what could have been a bitter, divisive all-out floor fight on the issue between Chicago and downstate forces."

The summing up was interesting and possibly significant:

> The Bill of Rights was expected to provide explosive debate and prove a serious threat to the convention's work product, particularly after Gertz was appointed committee chairman. Tho there were some anxious moments, the issues did not prompt the furor at Con-Con which many had anticipated.
>
> Most of the credit for that goes to the overall committee membership — delegates from all political, economic and social walks of life who worked well together and provided balance and judgment.
>
> Tho some clauses are provocative, most observers consider the proposed new Preamble and Bill of Rights a reasonable package containing a little something for everyone.[1]

Not many days before the people were to vote on the new constitution, Dorothy Clune of U.P.I. wrote an article about the bill of rights that was widely published in newspapers throughout the state. Better than any other article, in my judgment, it gave a fair account of what we had done and the atmosphere in which we had worked. Dorothy Clune wrote:

> Born of some tough compromises, the bill of rights in Illinois' proposed constitution has won approval from liberals and conservatives alike.

[1] John Elmer, "New Constitution Offers Something Old and New," *Chicago Tribune,* November 10, 1970.

There is some irony in this ideological agreement because no section of the constitution deals with more fundamental political and philosophic concepts than the bill of rights.

In it are contained statements relating to the place of the individual and the state in society, working definitions of freedom and provisions for all the "hardrock" rights such as due process of law, freedom to worship, speak and assemble.

"It is probably the best state constitution bill of rights in the nation," Elmer Gertz said.

"As a whole, it's a damned good bill of rights," Arthur Lennon said.

Gertz, a Chicago liberal, was chairman of the sixth Illinois constitutional convention's bill of rights committee.

Lennon, a "practical conservative" from Joliet, was a member of the committee and a highly effective debater at the convention.

"What makes the bill of rights so strong," Gertz said, is that "it moves us into the 20th century on many of the great questions, especially such things as discrimination."

The bill, rather than making general statements about the rights of all, explicitly bars discrimination in jobs, the sale or rental of property.

Discrimination on the basis of sex is prohibited as is discrimination on the basis of a handicap.

"These statements on discrimination represent the continuing process of refining freedom in America," Gertz said.

Lennon was not as enthusiastic as Gertz concerning the antidiscrimination provisions but with the possible exception of the one dealing with the handicapped, he was not overly critical of them either.

"What if a one-eyed man applies for a job as a pilot?" he asked of the section on the handicapped.

The antidiscrimination sections, Lennon said, do break new constitutional ground in that they define the proper relationships between individuals, not just between an individual and society as a whole.

"This is a new different concept but is it not necessarily bad," he said.

One area in which a liberal-conservative split forced a convention compromise was in the section dealing with privacy.

The liberals wanted a flat statement barring various kinds of electronic eavesdropping but the conservatives argued such a bar would hobble law enforcement at a time when the crime rate is steadily increasing.

In the end, con-con came up with a section saying that the people must be safe from "unreasonable" interceptions of conversations. It will be up to the courts to decide what unreasonable is.

Lennon appeared especially pleased that the current jury system in Illinois was kept intact.

There was a movement at con-con to make provision for smaller juries and to institute majority rule rather than unanimity in reaching convictions.

It was argued that these changes would reduce overloaded court dockets.

"No one anywhere has come up with a better system than the jury system we have now and I'm glad that the new bill of rights leaves it as it is," Lennon said.

Gertz is particularly proud of what he terms a "breakthrough" in the area of criminal fines.

The new bill of rights stipulates that no person may be imprisoned for failure to pay a fine unless the failure is "willful." The section provides that adequate time must be given to make payment, in installments if necessary.

"This removes a basic inequity in which the poor automatically go to jail because they cannot afford the fine and the rich stay free because they can," Gertz said.

Lennon, while agreeing with the theory behind the provision on fines, said it was more a legislative matter than a constitutional one and belonged in a state statute.

The one section which clearly shows the mark of downstate interests at the convention is that dealing with the right to bear arms.

This section grants to each citizen what was called by con-con critics an "unprecedented" right to own firearms and fears were expressed that the section would serve as a bar to effective gun control legislation.

However, many downstate delegates were adamant in their support of the section and won out over urban liberals and the Chicago organization of Mayor Richard J. Daley.

Sentiment against gun control in the rural downstate areas is expressed often and with strong feeling.

Both Gertz and Lennon were hopeful for passage of the new constitution.

Even with its flaws it is so much better than what we have now it would be a great mistake for the people to reject it," Gertz said.[2]

In the December 7, 1970, issue of the *Congressional Record*, Senator Charles H. Percy inserted a statement giving his views in favor of the new state constitution. He singled out the bill of rights for his special commendation. "The most outstanding part of the new constitution is its bill of rights — hailed by some as the best in any constitution of the 50 states."

Senator Stevenson, too, and Governor Ogilvie, Lieutenant Governor Simon, Attorney General Scott, Mayor Daley, all singled out the bill of rights for special praise. Some who otherwise opposed the charter (such as the State Federation of Labor) found the bill of rights praiseworthy.

Nothing gave me more joy than the letter that I received from President Witwer as the year 1970 neared its close. The convention was over, the new constitution had been approved by the people, and Witwer could appraise the results. He wrote to me:

> I will always take the greatest pride in your appointment as Chairman of the Bill of Rights Committee. I could not have made a better choice and you measured up to the most severe and demanding challenges in leading the committee and the convention into an excellent result.
>
> I feel that of all the things accomplished by the New Constitution, no article thrills me more than the Bill of Rights.

All the bruises were cured, all the hurts vanished when I read and re-read these words.

Chicago Today described the bill of rights as "the keystone of any constitution."

> In our view this is one of the best parts of the new Illinois charter, and is likely to become a model for other states planning to overhaul their constitutions. . . .
>
> The sum effect of all these provisions is to put the state's weight more strongly on the side of individual rights and dignity; to make sure that future governments must deal with the citizen as a person, not as any abstract figure whose freedoms can be expanded or re-

[2] Dorothy Clune, "Proposed Illinois constitution — Liberals, conservatives support the bill of rights," *Chicago Daily Law Bulletin*, December 3, 1970.

stricted as the state wishes. In our view that's what the word "freedom" is all about. If the constitution is adopted, Illinoisans can be proud of their bill of rights.[3]

The Bulletin of the Chicago Area Chapter of the National Association of Social Workers said: "The 1970 Constitution is a very good document, but of necessity is not a perfect one. It contains the most far-reaching Human Rights provisions of any State in the Union."

One little publication captured in a sentimental manner what the bill of rights means to many.

Betty Howard is the delightfully feminine delegate from St. Charles, who is also engaged in public relations. She had cosponsored, with Odas Nicholson, the women's rights proposal that ultimately became the section of the bill of rights that proscribed discrimination on account of sex. She delighted and surprised the chairman of the Bill of Rights Committee and, I hope, many others by sending out during the Christmas-New Year season a beautifully done pamphlet devoted to the bill of rights, with her three young children, their playhouses, and their toys as the backdrop. Betty had not been a member of our committee; she had served on the education committee. On the cover, portions of the preamble are proudly visible. On the inside appear these appropriate words:

"Mommy served this year as a Delegate to the State's Constitutional Convention which drafted a new constitution containing a Bill of Rights to meet the needs of the people of the state.

"As we enjoy these rights, we will all have a Merrier Christmas and a brighter New Year."

There followed, on succeeding pages, in the children's family settings, the texts of various sections of the bill of rights — 1 (inherent and inalienable rights), 4 (freedom of speech), 6 (searches, seizures, privacy, and interceptions), 8 (rights after indictment), 10 (self-incrimination and double jeopardy), 11 (limitation of penalties after conviction), 13 (trial by jury), 15 (right of eminent

[3] Editorial, "New bill of rights for Illinois," *Chicago Today,* December 3, 1970.

domain), 17 (no discrimination in employment and the sale or rental of property), 20 (individual dignity), 22 (right to arms), and 24 (rights retained). Both what was included and what was excluded were significant. Betty did not include the section for which she had fought so hard, proscribing discrimination on account of sex.

Albert Raby was not one of the loud voices either in committee or on the floor of the convention. He spoke so quietly at times that it was difficult hearing him. But he never hesitated to assert his convictions, even if he stood alone or with few others. He observed everything, sometimes in a far shrewder manner than one might have credited. It was therefore gratifying that when the convention was over, he summed up favorably as to the charter as a whole and enthusiastically as to the bill of rights in the *Hyde Park-Kenwood Voices,* saying:

> As many of you will recall, I went to the Illinois Constitutional Convention highly suspicious of the possible results. For example, I often said it was the wrong time to call a convention and that we would have an uphill battle protecting our constitutional rights, let alone expect advances. The most progressive thing might have been to keep the old constitution.
>
> I saw my role as primarily defensive, maintaining that view throughout the proceedings.
>
> It was also clear to all the independents that if the two major parties ever got together to make a deal, our bargaining power and ability to give leadership would be nil.
>
> Nonetheless, early signs gave reason for hope. First, there was a sizable number of highly competent independents. They not only helped raise the Convention's intellectual level and shored each other up, but also proved politically astute in their collective wisdom. The intellectual and political abilities of the entire convention, with exceptions, was generally high.
>
> In addition, the independents were given a sizable amount of power. Of the 11 committee chairmanships, three went to independents: Elmer Gertz the Bill of Rights Committee, Peter Tomei the Suffrage and Elections Committee and Wayne Whalen headed what proved to be one of the most politically sensitive committees, Style, Drafting and Submission (or SDS) Committee.
>
> The appointments, made by Convention President Samuel Witwer, were not accidental.

As to the final product, I believe we have an excellent new Bill of Rights. This could have been anticipated considering the committee's composition. Of its 15 members, 4 were black, 2 were well-known white civil libertarians and the balance included an exceptionally large number of decent human beings from which we needed only 2 votes to carry the committee — but we usually got 4 or 5. Thus we probably have the finest Bill of Rights proposal of any state.

We made several improvements in civil rights and criminal procedures without any negative law-and-order hysteria such as preventive detention.

Even as to the right to arms section, Raby was not too downcast, concluding:

One of the issues that many of us fought against unsuccessfully was the right to bear arms. I do not feel that it was a major defeat, for the right to bear arms is given on the one hand and taken away with the other. Given the provision's vagueness and public concern about guns, the state will increasingly find it necessary to control and probably ban hand guns. But what is really disturbing is the psychology and belief in guns shown by many who see them as the first and last line of defense against what they think is wrong with our society.[4]

It would be wrong to sum up the preamble and bill of rights solely in terms of what their proponents in and out of the convention believed. While I feel strongly in agreement with those who praise our product as probably the best bill of rights in any state constitution (except possibly for a section or two), I know that measure and balance call for an expression of the views of those who, temperamentally or by reason of political and social principles, must necessarily be less than enthusiastic. One of the strong characters much to the right of the center was Dwight Friedrich, formerly a state senator from Centralia and one of the gadflies at the convention. A seat-mate of mine, we had many good-humored differences and more than a few that were basic indeed. I asked him to comment for this monograph, and he was good enough to reply:

Let me say at the outset that I felt, and I am sure that most of the people in this area felt, that if there was anything good about

[4] "Con-Con Report: A Solid Bill of Rights Emerges," *Hyde Park-Kenwood Voices,* Vol. 5, no. 9 (October 1970).

the old Constitution it was the Bill of Rights and the Preamble to the Constitution. The Bill of Rights had been implemented through the years by Legislation and has been tested by the Courts and I think there was very little justification for feeling that anything further could be done from a constitutional standpoint to insure individual rights and equality. Now, having said that, I would like to go through the Constitution and comment on those sections where changes have been made and my feeling about those changes.

I think the new Preamble is definitely inferior to the old one in that it virtually mandates a welfare state. I think the people are entitled to protection of their rights: right to vote, the right for police protection, etc., and I think that if anything else they should be guaranteed opportunity. It seems to me that this Preamble is slanted in the direction of making the State the provider of food and clothing rather than the insurer of opportunity to earn them. Through the years with the interpretation of the Courts I am afraid the changes will encourage welfarism in our state government.

The next section I would like to comment on is Section 14 [imprisonment for debt]. The first sentence, of course, is taken verbatim from the old Constitution. The second sentence, however, is certainly something new and I think is more far-reaching than it appears on the surface. "No person shall be imprisoned for failure to pay a fine in a criminal case unless he has been afforded adequate time to make payment, in installments if necessary, and has willfully failed to make payment." [This was the amendment that had been proposed by Gertz, Raby, and Weisberg.] This will, in the majority of cases, eliminate the use of fines as penalty for conviction of a crime and if it can be said there is discrimination, this will discriminate against the responsible and those who have saved money who have attachable assets and will accrue to the benefit of the ne'er-do-well who under this section will really have no penalty for minor crimes. You do now have a new Federal Court decision to support your view. [Friedrich seems to have missed the point that the Supreme Court cases mandate what we anticipated in our amendment.]

I do not believe that there is any justifiable constitutional use for Sections 17, 18 and 19 [the nondiscrimination sections]. Certainly Illinois has provided by statute against discrimination in matters of employment and created the Fair Employment Practices Commission. Certainly discrimination in the sale or rental of property has been covered by statute and is presently about as strong as you can make it. [In this Friedrich is wholly mistaken. There is no open housing legislation in Illinois, only scattered and ineffective municipal ordinances.]

Section 18 on the discrimination on the basis of sex I think in the long run will not work for the benefit of women but will work against them. Certainly in Illinois a number of laws have been passed which protect women in certain types of employment: from long hours, from heavy work and so on; those laws will not be constitutional under this constitution. I think there will be new interpretations in matters of child support and other areas where women have advantages such as our divorce law and alimony laws; these will go down the drain. I am certainly convinced that the majority of women were not wanting any change in this whole area of the constitution or in the statute.

It is hard to argue against Section 19 because I think we all are sympathetic toward the handicapped but again I think this is going to be the basis for an unbelievable number of law suits brought by people who were not hired and the suit will be brought on the basis that they were being discriminated against because of some handicap. I think this again could better have been taken care of by Legislation.

Section 20 on individual dignity I think is superfluous and again I think will be the basis of law suits by someone who has been called a hillbilly or some other thing. I think in the long run it will tend to divide the people and point out the various religious, racial and ethnic groups and divide rather than unite the people.

I am aware that Section 22 [right to arms] is more than we had in the old Constitution but I think for all practical purposes it is meaningless. If there was one thing that the people I represented wanted, it was a strong section with regard to the right to own and bear arms. Certainly they all resent the present licensing law which for all practical purposes is nothing but a revenue bill and creates another government bureau. It does nothing to deter crime because the criminal who is about to commit a felony certainly is not going to be worried about whether or not his gun is registered. Another factor is all the countries where some totalitarian form of government has taken over, the first thing they did was confiscate arms. I really believe that we would have done a great favor to the people of Illinois if we had been able to put in a stronger section here to protect the people in this general area.

Section 23 The first sentence on fundamental principles is identical with the old one. The second sentence is one that I added because of an amendment of mine. I feel very strongly that at least in this one little place in the new constitution there is the suggestion that there is a need for individual responsibility and an obligation on the part of the individual to make self-government work. I am aware that this really does not mandate either the government or the individual to do anything but it certainly suggests responsibility of the individual is important.

Now, boiling this down, I guess I should be pleased that there aren't more changes than there were in the old Bill of Rights since I was for retaining the old one. I am disturbed again about the suggestion in the Preamble that this is going to be a welfare state. I am concerned about Section 14 which I think will eliminate fines as a basis for penalty for crimes and I am concerned that we were not able to get in a stronger right to arms section.

As is apparent from this narrative, Thomas C. Kelleghan was probably the most vocally and belligerently conservative member of the Bill of Rights Committee and of the convention as well. Others may have shared his views — Dwight Friedrich, for one; but no one had so articulated his differences as to create a consistently conservative philosophy. Kelleghan's placing of all delegates in three distinct voting blocs, cutting across party lines — traditionalists, independents, and radicals — will long be recalled. When I asked him after the convention was over and the constitution, which he had opposed, adopted, to give his views of the making of the bill of rights, he sent me a copy of his pamphlet, "How Will The New Constitution Affect You?" The answer, according to Kelleghan, is dreadful to contemplate. He thought the radicals, numbering by his count nineteen, had dominated the convention in the end. He did not name whom he thought of as such, but there can be no doubt that at the very least they included the three of us on the Bill of Rights Committee who had so often attempted to thwart him — Gertz, Raby, and Weisberg. He equated the Independents with the radicals; we should not be underestimated, he said; we represent a new threat to American liberties. This led him at once to the preamble. He found the new language neither appropriate nor accept-

able. Just as he had maintained on the floor of the convention, he
charged that the new language was taken verbatim from the defeated
New York preamble. "Only those who wish to alter the form and
structure of Illinois Government would even suggest that changes
be made" in the preamble, he said. He repeated what he had said
earlier about our reliance upon the state, rather than God, and that
the result was socialism. However pleased he was by the adoption
of section 24 of the bill of rights as to rights retained by the individual citizens, he feared that by the very next article on the powers
of government (not within the sphere of our committee), the state,
rather than the people, was made supreme.

Generally, he described what we had done as a bill of wrongs,
rather than a bill of rights. Most of the changes, he said, expand
the rights of convicted criminals at the expense of law abiding citizens. "The other changes impose on Illinois citizens the most restrictive laws in the area of discrimination in the entire nation." He
thought it incredible that convicted persons could be permitted to
pay fines in installments. "Undoubtedly the courts will be issuing
coupon books, or even credit cards, to convicted offenders." He objected to the provision on the rehabilitative nature of punishment
after conviction. "Criminals are not rehabilitated by coddling of
them," he declared. The new concept of punishment was really a
throwback, he said, to the discredited provisions on that subject in
the 1818 and 1848 constitutions; "both prisons and the death
penalty were absolutely necessary to preserve public order." He
objected to the equal protection of the law clause on the ground
that, innovatively, it gave felons such protection. In fact, this provision nowhere spells out any special rights for any group, notwithstanding Kelleghan; like the federal provision, it is applicable to
all persons. He objected also to our prohibition of unreasonable
invasions of privacy or interceptions of communications. He feared
that because of this provision "kidnapers, bombers, obscene phone
callers, false fire alarms in time of riot, gambling and so on" might
be uncontrolled. He made much of a comma; he thought it was
dangerous to permit "the right to assemble in a peaceable manner:
unless it was for the purpose of consulting for the common good or
to ask for redress of grievances." He was distressed by the provision
as to prompt preliminary hearings in certain criminal matters; he

thought it would harm the innocent! He thought the court calendars would be clogged because of the sections on nondiscrimination. Hence, we had created, as he said, a bill of wrongs against Illinois citizens.

Others have been quoted in praise and dispraise of the new Illinois preamble and bill of rights. It is not inappropriate or immodest for the chairman of the committee to have his personal say on the matter in the end. I think that I am relatively objective, at least sufficiently skeptical to be prepared for something less than complete satisfaction as to how the provisions may actually work out.

I have no basic quarrel with the sections that have been retained in the very verbiage of the 1870 constitution. This encompasses sections 1 (inherent and inalienable rights), 3 (religious freedom), 8 (rights after indictment), 10 (self-incrimination and double jeopardy), 16 (ex post facto laws and impairing contracts), and 21 (quartering of soldiers), and the two old sections transferred to the suffrage and elections article and the militia article. I am satisfied that the courts in the past have applied those sections properly and presumably will still do so in the future. Here and there I would have preferred verbal or even substantive improvements, but I am not too disappointed.

As to a few unchanged provisions, I still have misgivings. I feel strongly that the reference to truth in libel, contained in section 4 (freedom of speech), should have been modified or omitted in order to comply with federal constitutional standards laid down in *New York Times* v. *Sullivan*[5] and its growing progeny. I don't like a state constitution to flout the United States Supreme Court. I maintain that Illinois is not Mississippi.

I still feel that section 9 (bail and habeas corpus) should have been revised in order to express in unmistakable terms the goal of releasing accused persons before trial on little or no bail if it is demonstrably clear that they will appear for trial. I still subscribe to what Raby, Weisberg, and I said in our minority report on the subject. True, the situation may be corrected through legislation, but there can be no absolute assurance of this in practice.

[5] 376 U.S. 254 (1964).

As to the revised provisions, there is much that I can say in agreement, even where the revision did not go as I preferred.

I can have nothing but praise for our addition of equal protection of the laws to due process (section 2). We prevented a catastrophe when we succeeded in expurgating the phrase "including the unborn."

We strengthened section 5 (right to assemble and petition) when we removed the suggestion that some worthy purpose might be required for the right to assemble. While I did not oppose the Lawlor-Lennon addition of the phrase "to associate freely" I am grateful that the convention rejected that language as suggestive of exclusion in country club fashion, or worse.

Of course, I feel triumphant, in an almost delirious fashion, about the far-reaching nature of the revision of the search and seizure provisions, profoundly enhanced by the addition of the prohibition against unreasonable invasions of privacy or interceptions of communications (section 6). Suffice it to say that we in Illinois have rebuked Big Brother by this new language and have delayed 1984. In an age when people are dwarfed, stifled, and made to fear by the intrusions in their personal lives, it is good to know that our state has gone beyond any other in strengthening the privacy of the individual.

I do not know how much we have added by the inclusion in section 7 of the requirement for a prompt preliminary hearing in certain circumstances to establish probable cause in the case of a felony. I still think that it was necessary to constitutionalize what the statute purported to require since the actual practice seems to have repudiated the words of the statute. I am not completely satisfied. This is an area that will call for further revision, sooner or later, either by a constitutional amendment or a statute. The provision as to the grand jury must also be reviewed periodically.

One of our great potential achievements with respect to section 11 (limitation of penalties after conviction) is the concept that penalties "shall be determined both according to the seriousness of the offense and with the objective of restoring the offender to useful citizenship." This is good. In each and every case, we ought to go beyond the punitive. Recognizing that it was not our intent thereby to abolish capital punishment, this may still be the effect in the long run. For you cannot rehabilitate an executed person. Needless to say, I regret the defeat of the separate submission on the abolition of the death penalty; and I regret that there was a separate submission. My originial impulse against including anything on the subject was right. I let excessive optimism run away with me. I can only plead that I sinned on the side of the angels.

The revision of section 12 (right to remedy and justice) may prove to be more significant than some believe. I think the mandatory language gives the provision much more meaning than it has had in the past; and I applaud the inclusion of privacy as a protected right. It adds to the private sector what section 6 assured as to the state and its minions. Everything that protects the individual is all to the good, especially in a period that is obsessed with false notions as to law-and-order.

While cognizant of the disgracefully crowded nature and delays of the civil trial calendar in Cook County, and sympathetic to the views expressed by Chief Justice Underwood, I am still happy that we retained unimpaired the right of trial by jury (section 13). I think the many problems can be solved without tampering with the ancient institution that has given such protection to all of us. The principal reason for the delays in Cook County is the growing number of personal injury cases. This problem should be attacked directly in some fashion, inappropriate in this place to discuss in detail.

I am proud indeed that Raby, Weisberg, and I anticipated the United States Supreme Court decisions in this area, and advocated successfully in our minority report a revision of the provisions with respect to imprisonment for debt (section 14), so that the poor would not be punished doubly for their poverty. More money, rather than less, will be collected when fines can be paid in the more liberal fashion we provided in the revised section; and a segment of society already sensitive to its wrongs will not feel that it is forgotten in our system of criminal justice.

I do not think that we went far enough in our revision with respect to eminent domain (section 15), but it is a start towards a more just means of compensating for public taking of private property. How good or bad the section is will depend upon court interpretations in the future. The pressure of the representatives of public bodies was too great at the convention for us to have done more. At the very least, we have cleared away the old incumbrances as to railroads.

The sections as to nondiscrimination (sections 17, 18, and 19) are the most far-reaching of all of the new provisions in the bill of rights. I am proud indeed that we in Illinois have gone beyond all the other states and the federal government in eliminating discrimination in the more important areas — employment and the sale or rental of property. We have added to the rights of all persons, regardless of adventitious circumstances like race, color, creed, national ancestry, sex, and physical and mental handicap. This is all the more remarkable in view of the failures of the legislature. The virtual unanimity with which the convention acted, and the failure to mount a campaign against the constitution because of these basic new rights, are remarkable indeed.

Of course, I have misgivings as to the provision on individual dignity (section 20). Most of the time, in committee and in general session at the convention, I refrained from voting either way. In the end, I voted for the section as a gesture of unity. I know that my fellow libertarians were much disappointed when I failed to vote a resounding no. I do not feel that this section impairs freedom of expression; at least our committee report and the debate in and out of committee indicated that. I feel strongly enough against the nasty and vicious habit of stereotyping and maligning people to welcome a constitutional sermon against it. What is wrong with telling bigots they are wrong, if you don't create a cause of action in the process? I am not dogmatic about the answer even if those I most admire won't like it. Hence I don't regard this section as a blot on our record, even if I would not have wept at its exclusion.

I still regret and resent the provision on the so-called right to arms (section 22), even if it is hemmed in with the protective police power. It is morally wrong, I feel, to give aid and comfort, however limited, to those who can do violence. I want to create a peaceful society, and this is a reprehensible way of avoiding it. I stand back of all that was said by Raby, Weisberg, and myself in our minority report. This is a document that may yet haunt the delegates responsible for the first forced tribute to the gun-toters.

And this suggests that it was wise, both in principle and strategy, to add to section 23 (fundamental principles) a reminder about the need for individual obligations and responsibilities.

Finally, I am glad that we recognized in section 24 (rights retained) that by enumerating certain rights, we did not intend "to deny or disparage others retained by the individual citizens of the State." The more individual rights there are, the better for all of us and for the state.

When one recalls the fear that many of us had, reasonably I think, that the bill of rights might be so regressive as to warrant the defeat of any new constitution, one is ready to stand up and cheer, as I do, the new charter of basic rights. From its resounding preamble to its last section, it is largely good, overwhelmingly virtuous. It does have within it the potential, expressed in the new words included in the preamble to "eliminate poverty and inequality; assure legal, social and economic justice; provide opportunity for the fullest development of the individual. . . ." What more can one expect of a bill of rights? For our day and the first hours of tomorrow, we have achieved enough.

Index